Langenscheidt

Englisch

Typische Fehler vermeiden

Ein unterhaltsamer Ratgeber
zur richtigen Wortwahl

Von Dr. Sonia Brough
und Carolyn Kilday Wittmann

Langenscheidt

Berlin · München · Wien · Zürich · New York

Umwelthinweis: gedruckt auf chlorfrei gebleichtem Papier

Umschlaggestaltung: Independent Medien-Design
Zeichnungen im Innenteil: Alfred Taubenberger

Druck: Druckhaus Langenscheidt KG, Berlin-Schöneberg
Printed in Germany
ISBN 3-468-**29901**-X
www.langenscheidt.de

2. 3. 4. 5. * 05 04 03 02

Inhalt

Vorwort

Da fehlen einem doch glatt die Worte! Hat man mit Müh und Not jede Menge Wortschatz eingepaukt, greift man doch immer wieder in die falsche Schublade: Diese verflixten deutschen Wörter, die im Englischen zwei, drei, vier oder noch mehr Entsprechungen haben. „Platz", zum Beispiel. Heißt das nun *room*, *space* oder *place* oder aber *seat*, wenn nicht gar *square*? Ganz schön verwirrend, nicht wahr?

Aber mit diesem Buch werden Sie sich schnell wieder zurechtfinden. Das richtige Wort am richtigen Platz – pardon, an der richtigen Stelle – das ist unser Ziel.

Kurz zum Aufbau des Buches: Jedes Stichwortkapitel besteht aus drei Teilen:

① Eine Anekdote oder illustrierte Beispielsätze, in denen die kniffligen Wörter vorgestellt werden.
② Eine genaue Erklärung, in der diese Wörter unter die Lupe genommen werden. Hierbei helfen wiederum typische Beispielsätze sowie auch Eselsbrücken.
③ Zur Abrundung ein kleiner Test mit ganz typischen Anwendungsbeispielen, mit deren Hilfe Sie Ihre soeben erworbenen Kenntnisse überprüfen und festigen können.

Wir raten Ihnen, beim Durcharbeiten der Erklärungen immer wieder auf den Ausgangstext zurückzublicken, um sich mit den jeweiligen Begriffen vertraut zu machen. Beim Test sollten Sie dann ruhig sowohl die Erklärungen als auch den Text zu Rate ziehen. Durch das Zusammenspiel dieser drei Bestandteile werden Sie auf amüsant-anschauliche Weise sicher ans Ziel geführt – treffsichere Wortwahl statt Qual der Wahl mit womöglich peinlichen Fehltritten.

Übrigens: Wir haben viele der behandelten Wörter an anderen Stellen „hineingeschmuggelt", um deren Gebrauch noch mehr zu festigen. Darüber hinaus werden Sie auf jede Menge aktuelles Vokabular stoßen und somit Ihren Wortschatz noch mehr erweitern.

Die Auswahl der Problemfälle ist natürlich nicht erschöpfend. Wir haben ganz gezielt eine Reihe von Begriffen ausgesucht, mit denen gerade Deutschsprachige ihre Schwierigkeiten haben. Um Ihnen jeweils das Kernproblem vor Augen zu halten, haben wir dann und wann eine vereinfachte Darstellung gern in Kauf genommen.

Ein Tipp noch: Besser jeden Tag ein halbes Stündchen als eine lange Wochenendorgie – das bringt wesentlich mehr. Und vergessen Sie nicht: Es ist nicht mit einem Mal getan – beim Sprachenlernen liegt in der **Wiederholung** der Schlüssel zum Erfolg. Wir wünschen Ihnen dabei viel Spaß!

Autoren und Verlag

Hinweise für den Leser:
Die im Text verwendeten Symbole haben folgende Bedeutung:

Wo dieses Symbol erscheint, soll Ihnen ein Licht aufgehen. Es weist auf eine „Eselsbrücke" hin, die Ihnen helfen soll, sich etwas Wichtiges zu merken.

Dieses Warndreieck bedeutet „Vorsicht!". Hier wird auf eine besonders tückische Fehlerquelle hingewiesen, auf die Sie Acht geben sollten.

Dieser Bleistift zeigt Ihnen, dass Sie jetzt dran sind. Hier können Sie Ihre Kenntnisse testen.

Dieser entsetzte „Smiley" erscheint hin und wieder, wenn Helmut, einer der Hauptdarsteller in diesem Buch, einen gravierenden Englisch-Fehler begangen hat. Sie sollten Helmut in solchen Fällen tunlichst nicht nachahmen!

Abkürzungen:

Am.	amerikanisch	*o.s.*	oneself
Brit.	britisch	*pl.*	Plural, Mehrzahl
bes.	besonders	*s.o.*	someone
bzw.	beziehungsweise	*s.th.*	something
jd.	jemand(en)	*umgs.*	umgangssprachlich
jdm.	jemandem	*usw.*	und so weiter
jds.	jemandes	*vgl.*	vergleiche

Typische Fehler von A–Z

aufstehen

get up? | **stand up?**

*Helmut always **gets up** late when he's in England.*

aus dem <u>Bett</u> aufstehen (und sich fertig machen):

get up

kann <u>nicht</u> durch *stand up* ersetzt werden

*Being a gentleman, Helmut **stood up** to give Sally his seat.*

sich vom Stuhl, Sofa usw. <u>erheben</u>:

stand up

kann auch mit ***get up*** ausgedrückt werden

Im Zweifelsfall nehmen Sie ***get up***, denn das deckt beide Fälle ab. Wenn ***from*** + „Sitzgelegenheit" folgt, **muss** man sogar ***get up*** nehmen:
*He **got up from** the **sofa** straightaway.*

stand up wird eher in formellen Situationen bevorzugt:
The class stood up as the headmistress came in.

Und falls Sie nach dem „Aufstehen“ noch nicht ganz munter sein sollten, hier ein kleiner Test:

get up *oder* ***stand up?*** *Setzen Sie die passende Form ein.*

1. *If you _________________ now, you might get some breakfast before it's all gone.*

2. *In British cinemas most people don't _________________ for the national anthem any more.*

Bank

bank? **bench?**

This is probably the nearest Fred will ever get to a ***bank account*** *– sleeping on an uncomfortable* ***bench*** *in front of the* ***bank****. You may feel sorry for him, but actually he's happier here than he was in prison a few months ago, slaving away at a* ***work bench****. But he'd better be careful, otherwise he might appear before the* ***magistrate's bench*** *again, and that would be the end of his life in the open.*

---

work bench – Werkbank ***appear before the magistrate's bench*** – vor den Kadi („die Richterbank") kommen

bank

Geldinstitut

I've just opened a savings account at Lloyd's Bank in the High Street.

bank holiday – gesetzlicher Feiertag (an dem in erster Linie die Banken geschlossen bleiben)

bench

Sitzbank, auch übertragen in Verbindung mit verschiedenen Berufen

substitutes' bench – Reservebank
backbencher – Hinterbänkler

After jogging for an hour he was glad to have a rest on the park bench.
It often takes years for young MPs to make their way from the back to the front benches.

bank oder ***bench?***

1. *It can be very frustrating for a footballer to have to sit on the substitutes' ________________ for weeks on end.*
2. *If you need traveller's cheques, you'd better order them at the ________________ soon.*
3. *Ever since Parliament allowed television to broadcast debates, there has been less newspaper-reading and falling asleep on the back ________________ (pl.).*

bemerken

notice? **remark?**

*I couldn't help **noticing** that he had odd socks on.*

*I **remarked** that I liked his shoes very much.*

notice

mit den Augen/Ohren usw. bemerken, wahrnehmen
I noticed – mir ist aufgefallen
Did you notice that funny notice on the notice-board?

remark

(gehoben) mündlich bemerken, sagen
She remarked how much she liked my new curtains.
Statt des gehobenen *remark* sagt man meist ganz einfach ***say***.
remark mit dem ***Mund***, sonst ***notice***

---

notice – Anschlag ***notice-board*** – schwarzes Brett

***notice** oder **remark?** Setzen Sie die passende Form ein.*

When she ________________ me slipping in through the door half an hour late, she loudly ________________ that she was a great believer in punctuality.

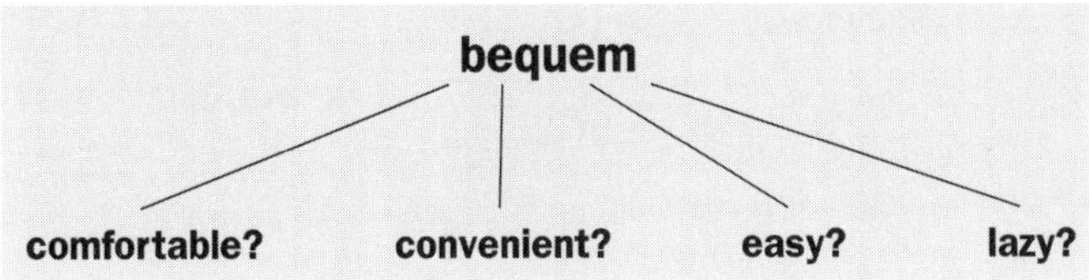

The easy way out

The nearest shops to my house are over a mile away, so it's either a question of putting on ***a comfortable pair of shoes*** *and walking half an hour to the shopping centre, or taking* ***the easy way out*** *and using the car. In time, of course, you get very* ***lazy*** *and fill your freezer and pantry with convenience foods. I do draw the line at TV dinners, however. It may be* ***convenient*** *to sit back in* ***a comfortable armchair*** *eating a meal which took you three minutes to heat up in the microwave, but I must admit even my dog turned his nose up at the lasagna I offered to share with him during "Dallas" the other evening.*

comfortable

bequem, was das körperliche Wohlbefinden angeht
I wish we had more comfortable chairs to sit on in the office.

convenient

sehr praktisch, keine Umstände verursachend
It's so convenient living in the town centre with so many shops and restaurants nearby.

easy

einfach, mühelos, ohne viel körperlichen oder geistigen Aufwand
He's made life very easy for himself by just sending his children to boarding school.

lazy

faul, bequem
Sometimes he's too lazy to get up and answer the phone.

12 **comfortable, convenient, easy** oder **lazy?**

1. *The new flat's very ________________ as far as public transport goes – there are bus stops and a Tube station just down the road.*

2. *Sit down and make yourself ________________.*

3. *I know everybody thinks that civil servants are ________________ and lead a very ________________ life. They ought to try my job at the Department of the Environment.*

4. *As Margaret says, there are no ________________ solutions to difficult problems.*

---

civil servant – Beamter ***Department of the Environment*** – Umweltministerium

besondere(r,-s)

special? **particular?**

Mr Wilson: *As it's your birthday, I've decided to give you a* ***special treat*** *and take you out for a meal and then to the cinema. Is there* ***any particular film*** *you'd like to see?*
Mrs Wilson: *It's not like you to be so generous, Norman. Are you making a* ***special effort*** *because you forgot our wedding anniversary last month?*
Mr Wilson: *No, there's no* ***particular reason*** *– except that you're a very* ***special person*** *...*

give s.o. a special treat – jdm. eine besondere Freude machen

Dies ist schon ein besonderer Fall *(a special case)*, denn die Unterschiede zwischen *special* und *particular* sind besonders fein *(particularly subtle)* und verlangen daher Ihre besondere Aufmerksamkeit *(your special attention)*.

special

1. außergewöhnlich, nicht alltäglich, Sonder ...
   a special person/case/event
   What's so special about this restaurant?
2. speziell, Sonder ...
   special training/treatment
   a special technique

particular

(ganz) bestimmte(r,-s) aus einer Reihe von Möglichkeiten; man stellt sich dabei meist etwas ganz Konkretes vor
"I'm looking for a couch." – "Have you got any particular style in mind?"

special oder **particular?**

I want to get Nick something ______________ *for his eighteenth birthday, and there's one* ____________ *video camera he's keen on. My sister knows a dealer who might give me a* ____________ *price.*

be keen on – „scharf" sein auf

besuchen

go and see?/(pay s.o. a) visit? **go to?/attend?**

It's a busy life

Mrs Wilson: *When was the last time you* ***paid your Auntie Flora a visit****, Peter?*

Peter: *Oh, Mum, I'm too busy to* ***go and see all these relatives****. On Monday evenings I've got sports, and on Tuesdays and Thursdays I* ***go to my Japanese class****. Mr Honda says he expects us to* ***attend the course*** *regularly if we want to* ***go to Kyoto University*** *for our year abroad. That just leaves a bit of free time at the weekends for me to see my friends. Anyway, why don't you go and* ***visit*** *Auntie Flora – she is your sister, after all.*

go and see s.o.

(auch ***go to see s.o.***) jd. besuchen
I must go and see my parents tomorrow.

pay s.o. a visit

jd. besuchen, jdm. einen Besuch abstatten; gehobener als *go and see*
You really ought to pay poor Mr Trump a visit.

visit s.o.

jd. besuchen, oft auf offizieller Ebene, zu bestimmten Besuchszeiten oder aus Verpflichtung
Will you come and visit me when I'm in jail?

go to

(die Schule/Universität, einen Kurs usw.) regelmäßig besuchen
I go to body-building classes every night. Which school did you go to?

attend

1. (an einem Kurs, einer Klasse usw.) teilnehmen; gehobener als *go to*
   Pupils who are unable to attend a class must provide a written excuse.
2. (gehoben) (eine Schule usw.) besuchen
   Please list all schools and institutions of higher education you have attended.

go and see, visit, go to *oder* **attend?** *Setzen Sie die passende Form ein.*

1. *Does your little boy still ________________ kindergarten?*

2. *Foreign ministers from all the EC countries are expected to ________________ next month's conference.*

3. *I must ________________ my sister this weekend – she's been in bed with an awful cold.*

4. *The Archbishop of Canterbury is to ________________ the Pope in February.*

bis (zu)

until/till? | **by?** | **by the time?**

Ups and downs

Mr Wilson: *I wish they'd hurry up.* ***By the time they get us out*** *of this lift the meeting will be over; and I'm supposed to be home* ***by eight at the latest*** *for a dinner party. My wife will kill me if I keep everyone waiting again.*
Mr Smithers: *Well, it's a good thing there's an emergency phone at least. I certainly wouldn't fancy being stuck in this lift with you* ***till tomorrow morning****, Mr Wilson.*
Mr Wilson: *If you carry on talking to me in that tone, Smithers, you'll be out of a job* ***by the end of the year****.*

until/till

werden bei einer ununterbrochenen **Zeitdauer** benutzt;
Zustand/Tätigkeit bleiben unverändert
We danced till three o'clock in the morning.

by, by the time

bis spätestens, bis endlich;
beziehen sich auf einen Zeitpunkt oder Termin, vor dem etwas geschehen muss(te) usw.

by + Zeitangabe:
I've got to hand this seminar paper in ***by the 28th****.* (Frist/Termin)
We should have been in Alice Springs ***by Friday****.* (Zeitpunkt)

by the time + Verbkonstruktion:
By the time you've finished *packing, the plane will have left without us.* (Zeitpunkt)

By the time he called *I had left the office.* (Zeitpunkt)
I want you to be in bed ***by the time I get home.*** (Termin)

until 12 o'clock

– – – – – > – – – – – > – – – – – > – – – – – > – – – – – > – –

I'll be working until twelve.

?　　　?　　　?

10.30　　*11.15*　　*11.50*　　***by 12 o'clock!***

– – – – – × – – – – – – × – – – – – – × – – – – – – – – – – –

She'll be back by twelve.

Übrigens: *See you later!* – Bis später!

until, by *oder* ***by the time?***

1. *Could you have the flat cleaned and the dinner ready ____________ six o'clock?*

2. *You're going to stay here ________________ you've sobered up.*

3. *________________ I realized who it was, it was too late to ask for an autograph.*

---

sober up – (wieder) nüchtern werden

Boden

ground? **floor?**

Organic gardening

*"What's all this soil doing on my **kitchen floor**, Jimmy?"*
*"Well, I'm trying to breed worms, Mum, but if I do it on the **ground outside** they all crawl away. When I've got enough, I'll put them back into your vegetable bed to make your carrots and cauliflower taste better."*

---

organic gardening – biologischer Anbau ***breed*** – züchten ***bed*** – Beet ***cauliflower*** – Blumenkohl

Nach diesem tapferen Versuch des Jung-Ökologen Jimmy wollen wir unsererseits den „Boden" ein bisschen bearbeiten:

ground

Boden draußen, Grund
The ground's so hard, I can hardly get the spade into it.
We were stuck on the runway for hours before the plane got off the ground.
Übrigens: ***soil*** – lockerer Boden, Erdreich

floor

Fußboden im Haus
Why do the kids always leave their toys lying around on the floor?

floor = **Fußboden** – ***ground*** = **Grund**

ground *oder* ***floor?***

The ______________ is far too wet to let Jimmy and his pals sleep in the tent tonight. We'll just have to spread some mattresses out on the living-room ______________ and bed them down there.

---

pal – Freund, „Spezi" ***bed s.o. down*** – jd. schlafen legen

brauchen

need? **take?**

City life

***It takes** the average commuter up to two hours **to** get home in the evening rush-hour. At times the traffic almost comes to a standstill. What we **need** is a more efficient public transport system, or we should introduce more flexible working hours so that everyone isn't travelling to and from work at the same time. I can't understand why **it's taking** the politicians so long **to** find a solution to the problem of our congested roads. Perhaps they **need** a nine-to-five job just to see how the other half lives.*

---

commuter – Pendler ***flexible working hours*** – gleitende Arbeitszeit ***congested*** – verstopft ***the other half*** – wir Normalbürger

need

benötigen
This hoover is falling apart – we definitely need a new one.

take

(Zeit, Energie usw.) in Anspruch nehmen, um ein bestimmtes Ziel zu erreichen; betont den Aufwand und wird meist durch *it* eingeleitet
It took him years of hard work to get where he is today.

Übersetzen Sie:

1. *Ich brauche eine Krawatte für die Hochzeit.*
2. *Er braucht nur zehn Minuten, um eine Seite zu tippen.*
3. *Wie lange hast du gebraucht, um hier herzukommen?*

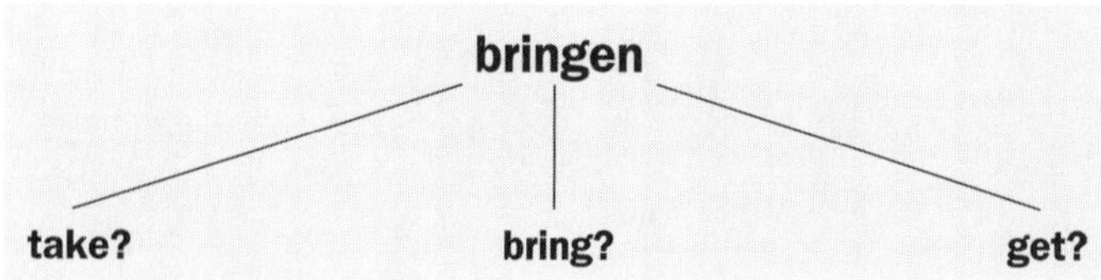

The fun and games are over

*If you **get** me the timetable, we can work out when I have to **take** you to the station. And don't forget to **take** your grandmother some flowers when you go to fetch the dog. And another thing, Peter – next time you come home, please don't **bring** all your friends at the same time.*

take

(irgendwohin) bringen
(vom Standort des Sprechers oder Handelnden weg)
Could you take these empty boxes into the cellar?

bring

herbringen (zum Standort des Sprechers oder Entgegennehmenden her); oft in der Konstruktion *bring s.o. s.th.*
Bring me my slippers, will you?

get

(her)bringen, holen;
meist in der Konstruktion *get s.o. s.th.*
Get him a glass of water, quick!

take, bring *oder* ***get?*** *Setzen Sie die passende Form ein.*

1. *The ambulance ________________ him straight to hospital, and he was operated on immediately.*

2. *I'm too lazy to get up – can you ________________ me my glasses from the desk?*

3. *Don't forget to ________________ your swimming trunks when you come and see us.*

Who's the boss around here?

Sally: *I think you'd make a good **chef**, Helmut.*
Helmut: *Really?*
Sally: *Well, you're good at planning, you can coordinate things, work under pressure, and you always have everything ready in time.*
Helmut: *Yes, I can just see myself running a huge department in a multinational company ...*
Sally: *I said **chef**, Helmut, not **boss**. I'm talking about working in a kitchen, not in some big firm. Actually, perhaps you ought to spend less time with your nose in the cooking pots and stick it into your English vocabulary book more often.*
Helmut: *Whatever you say, **boss**.*

Ist Ihnen klar geworden, was Helmut durcheinander gebracht hat? Die folgenden Erklärungen geben Aufschluss.

boss

(leicht umgs.) Chef;
einen neutralen Allgemeinausdruck für „Chef" gibt es nicht; mögliche Übersetzungen sind:
head of department, supervisor, manager, managing director usw.

Wenn die genaue Funktion unbekannt ist, kann man *person in charge* sagen.

Look out, here comes the boss. We'd better get back to work.

Übrigens:
boss s.o. around – jd. herumkommandieren
bossy – herrisch

chef

Küchenchef, Chefkoch
He says he's chef of a three-star restaurant.

chief

Häuptling
You look like an Indian chief with all those feathers in your hat.

boss

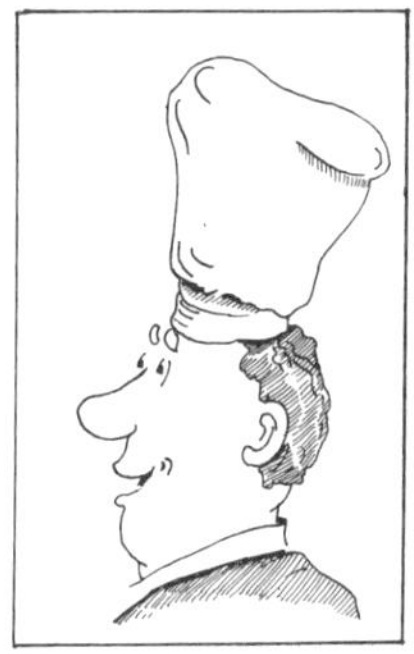

chef

chief

boss *oder* **chef?**

1. *My compliments to the ________________ – the roast lamb was excellent.*
2. *The new ________________ is starting tomorrow, and everybody in the office is really nervous.*

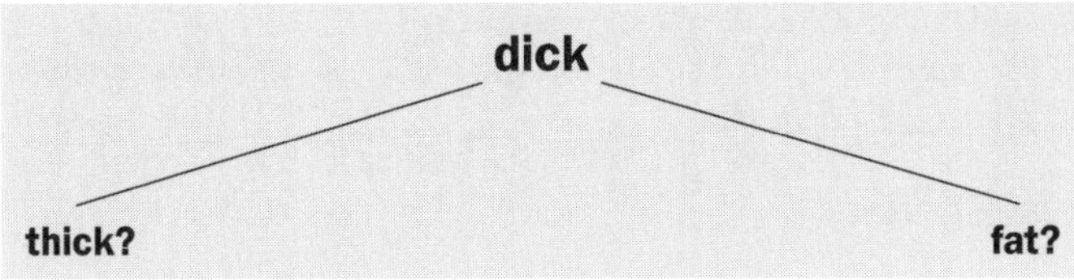

With friends like you, who needs enemies?

One Sunday afternoon Helmut was playing Scrabble with the Wilsons and was collecting quite a lot of points. Just as he was putting down another four-letter word, Sally came in. Helmut knew that she had been trying to lose weight, so he decided to pay her a compliment. "Hello Sally," he said with his usual charming smile, "You're not as thick as you used to be!" ☹ Everyone looked at him, and Sally's brother Peter said very defensively, "Actually, Sally has always been quite clever – in fact, she's probably the most intelligent person in this room." That was when Helmut realized that he must have said something wrong …

Scrabble – „Scrabble", eine Art Wortbildungsspiel

Ja, hier ist unser Helmut voll ins Fettnäpfchen getreten, denn: *thick* bedeutet bei Personen keineswegs „dick", sondern „blöd", „schwer von Begriff". Was er gemeint hat, war natürlich *fat*, aber auch das wäre etwas plump gewesen. Da wäre *plump* (= mollig) schon angebrachter. Aber um Sally ein echtes Kompliment zu machen, hätte er eigentlich sagen müssen: *You're much slimmer than you used to be.* Das Kästchen wird Sie vor ähnlichen „dicken Hunden" bewahren.

fat

dick, fett
He's almost too fat to get through the front door.

thick

1. (Buch, Stoff, Suppe usw.) dick
   This material is too thick for a summer dress.

2. (sehr umgs.!) blöd, schwer von Begriff
He must be a bit thick if he can't tell the difference between French and English.

thick *oder* ***fat?***

My wife thinks I'm much too ________________, so for my birthday she gave me a ________________ book on how to lose weight and an expensive cashmere suit that's three sizes too small for me. She obviously thinks I'm stupid, but I'm not that ________________.

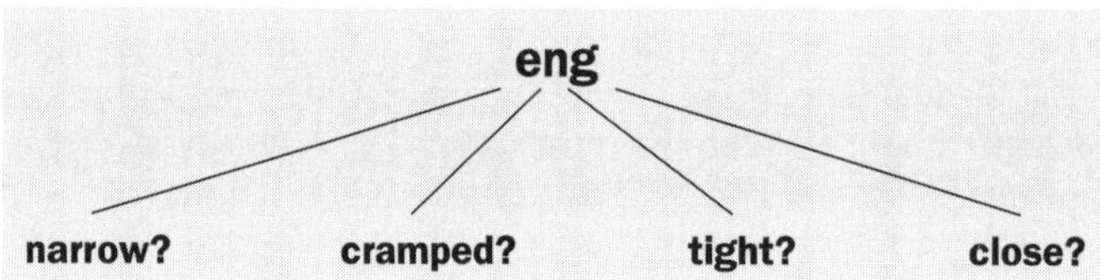

You're cramping my style

Helmut: *Sally, I know you like* ***narrow skirts****, but don't you think the one you wore to the party last night was a bit too* ***tight****?*
Sally: *Don't be so narrow-minded, Helmut – it's the fashion. I'm more worried about my new shoes. They're such a* ***tight fit****, they really hurt.*
Helmut: *I also thought you and John were sitting very* ***close together*** *on the sofa.*
Sally: *I do believe you're jealous, Helmut. The* ***flat*** *was so* ***cramped****, there was nowhere else to sit. Anyway, John and I have been* ***close friends*** *for years.*
Helmut: *It's not that I want to cramp your style, but I did take you to the party after all …*

---

cramp someone's style – jd. einengen

Helmut hat wohl die ganze Sache ein bisschen zu eng gesehen. Wir müssen auf jeden Fall etwas in die Breite gehen, um dem breiten Spektrum dieses kleinen Wörtchens gerecht zu werden.

narrow

1. schmal, eng (Gegenteil: breit)
   We spent hours walking through the narrow, busy streets and alleyways of the old city.
2. (im übertragenen Sinn) eng, begrenzt
   He takes a very narrow view of the matter.
   narrow-minded – engstirnig

cramped

räumlich eng, beengend
He hates cooking in the cramped kitchen.
Many refugees are living in cramped and filthy conditions.

tight

eng sitzend/anliegend, oft zu eng/fest
I must have put on weight – these trousers were never so tight before.

close

1. ***close to*** – eng an, dicht an/neben
   close together – dicht nebeneinander, eng aneinander
2. (Beziehungen, Kontakte) eng
   We're still in close contact.

narrow, cramped, tight *oder* ***close?***

1. *It's so ______________ in this flat, there's hardly any room to move.*

2. *What we need is ______________ cooperation between environmentalist groups.*

3. *Oh Mum, you're a bit behind the times – these jeans are supposed to be ______________.*

4. *She's very ______________-minded about foreigners.*

erkennen

recognize? **realize?**

Fat and happy?

When they told me I had to put on 25 pounds for my role in the new film, I thought it would be great fun. But shortly after I started eating all those fried breakfasts and high-calorie desserts I ***realized*** *I would have to buy a lot of new clothes. After a month of pigging myself, I looked a different person. When my boyfriend got back from his business tour of the States he hardly* ***recognized me****. When he threatened to leave me if I didn't get back down to my normal weight very quickly, I* ***realized*** *that perhaps I had got things slightly out of proportion.*

pig o.s. – sich den Bauch voll schlagen ***get s.th. out of proportion*** – etwas übertreiben

recognize

1. wiedererkennen
   I hardly recognized you in those strange glasses.
2. (sehr gehoben) zur Kenntnis nehmen
   We do recognize the need for reform.
   (wird im Alltagsenglisch relativ selten benutzt)

realize

I realized – mir wurde klar, mir leuchtete ein
I soon realized it would be cheaper to rent a flat than to buy one.

recognize *oder* ***realize?*** *Setzen Sie die passende Form ein.*

1. *I wish they would ________________ that they can't learn English unless they make a proper effort.*

2. *John's smashed the car, I'm afraid. You won't ________________ it – it's a complete write-off.*

---

make an effort – sich bemühen/anstrengen ***write-off*** – Totalschaden

erst

only? **not until?**

First things first

Sally: *Helmut, you've* ***only*** *written three lines of your English essay so far.*
Helmut: *Yes, but it's* ***only*** *eight o'clock, and I do****n't*** *have to hand it in* ***until*** *tomorrow afternoon. I'm not really in the mood, anyway. Shall I take you down to the pub for a drink?*
Sally: ***Not until*** *you've done at least a page. What's it about, by the way?*
Helmut: *The title is "Are men really more domineering than women?".*

I'm not in the mood – ich habe keine Lust ***domineering*** – herrschsüchtig

only

1. nur, erst (es ist weniger/früher usw. als erwartet)
   I lent you ten pounds, and you've only given me three back.
   It's only ten past six and we've got the whole evening ahead of us.

   Oft in der Konstruktion *only … so far*
   We've only interviewed three candidates so far.
2. nicht eher / nicht früher als; betont den Zeitpunkt (häufig in der Vergangenheit)
   I only got back on Wednesday.

not until

nicht eher / nicht früher als, nicht (be)vor; betont die Zeitdauer, bis etwas eintritt (häufig in Bezug auf die Zukunft)
The party isn't tonight, it's not until next week.

Erst wenn Sie sich diese Unterschiede klar gemacht haben, sollten Sie das nächste Stichwort in Angriff nehmen; oder anders ausgedrückt:
Don't go on to the next item until you've really understood this one (and done the test, of course)!

Übersetzen Sie:

1. *Das Mittagessen wird erst um zwei fertig sein.*

2. *Der Scheck ist erst vorgestern angekommen.*

3. *Er wird erst nächstes Jahr fünfzig.*

4. *Sie haben erst ein Spiel gewonnen.*

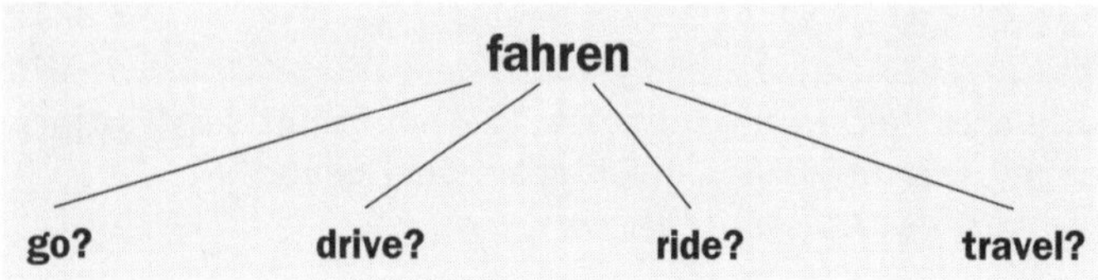

It's all go!

I hate ***driving to work*** *every morning – even with all these car pools the traffic jams don't seem to have got any better. So I'm considering* ***going by public transport****. But of course you've always got to reckon with strikes, and* ***travelling all that way*** *on the crowded London underground could be quite nerve-racking, too. Perhaps I should get myself a motorbike and* ***ride*** *to work* ***on*** *that.* ***Travelling*** *to and from work is sometimes more difficult than work itself. No wonder my husband has decided to opt out of the rat race and go in for desktop publishing at home.*

---

car pool – Fahrgemeinschaft ***nerve-racking*** – nervenaufreibend ***opt out*** – aussteigen ***rat race*** – Hektik des Berufsalltags

go

die geläufigste Übersetzung von „fahren“, ohne die Art des Fortkommens zu nennen
I'm going to Manchester tomorrow for a job interview.

Mit Betonung auf das Verkehrsmittel:
go by car/bus/train/underground/motorbike usw.
(antwortet auf die Frage „wie?“)

Alternativ hierzu:
take the car/bus/train/boat usw.

drive

1. (selbst) mit dem Auto usw. fahren (betont die Art des Transports bzw. die Fahrtätigkeit)
   You're not too old to learn to drive.
2. (ein Auto usw.) steuern, lenken, fahren
   I don't know how you manage to drive that old jeep.
3. (jd.) fahren, im Auto usw. mitnehmen
   It'll be easier if I drive you there.

ride

1. ([ein] Fahrrad oder Motorrad) fahren
   ride a bicycle/bike/motorbike
2. ***ride on a bus / on the underground / on a motorbike*** usw.
   mit dem Bus / der U-Bahn / dem Motorrad usw. fahren (betont die Art der Fortbewegung bzw. das Erlebnis)
   I love riding on the top of double-deckers.

travel

1. (eine meist lange Strecke) fahren; reisen
   We spent four weeks travelling through Greece.
   Richard hates travelling long distances.
2. ***travel on/by*** usw. – fahren mit
   She feels sick if she travels on buses, on the underground or by boat.

go, drive, ride *oder* ***travel?*** *Setzen Sie die passende Form ein.*

"Where are you __________ for your next holiday?" "Burgundy, although we can't decide how to __________ – whether to __________ by train or take the car. I don't particularly like __________, although you're more independent with the car, of course. We usually __________ long distances on the train, but I think this time Valerie would like us to have the car so that she can be __________ around from one Gothic cathedral to the next in comfort."

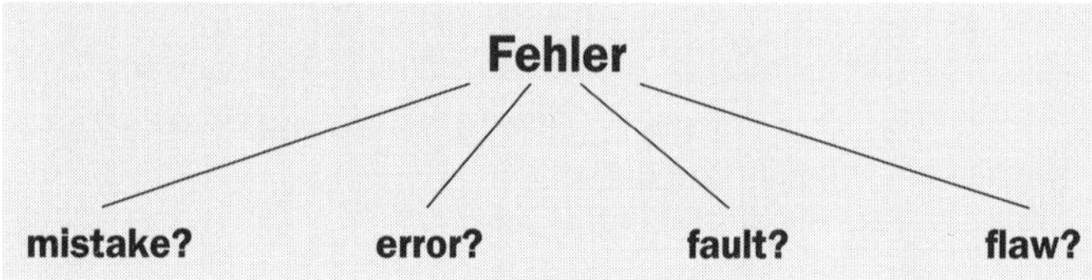

Checkmate

Secretary: *Yes, I'm afraid I made a* ***mistake****.*
Boss: *Made a* ***mistake****?! It was an absolute disaster!*
Secretary: *Well, I don't think it was my fault entirely. I am rather overworked, you know.*
Boss: *There's no excuse for it. To start with, there were at least 10* ***typing errors*** *in the letter – or were they perhaps* ***spelling mistakes****? And then you put it in the wrong envelope!*
Secretary: *Well, if the letter was so terrible, you should be glad Sir Harry never got it. In fact, I actually saved the situation.*
Boss: *There seems to be some* ***flaw in your argument****, Jane. And I refuse to keep putting your blunders down to human error. You're fired!*
Secretary: *I think you're making a big* ***mistake****, Mr Dobson. You see, I'll be paying my Uncle Harry a visit this weekend – it's his 90th birthday. And if you really want that £10,000 cheque for your new project …*

mistake

Fehler, Irrtum, Vergehen; die geläufigste Übersetzung
make a mistake – einen Fehler machen/begehen
spelling mistake – Rechtschreibfehler
Your homework is full of mistakes again.

error

Fehler, Irrtum; etwas gehobener als *mistake* und besonders in folgenden Kombinationen:
typing error – Tippfehler
printing error – Druckfehler (auch *misprint*)
Übrigens: *human error* – menschliches Versagen

fault

1. (technischer) Defekt, Materialfehler
   technical/electrical fault
   There seems to be a fault in the engine.
2. Schuld, Fehler (mit Schuldzuweisung verbunden)
   It's your fault. – Du bist schuld (daran).
   It's not my fault. – Ich kann nichts dafür.

flaw

1. Defekt, Materialfehler, Schwachstelle (meist nicht auf Anhieb ersichtlich)
   There's a flaw in this vase.
2. logischer Fehler/Schwachpunkt
   Whenever I make a new suggestion you find some flaw in it.
3. Charakterfehler
   It's just one of his many character flaws.

mistake, error, fault oder ***flaw?*** *(Try not to make any mistakes!)*

If I hadn't been up all night trying to decide whether there was a ________________ in the computer or the software, I wouldn't be making so many ________________ (pl.) *writing this letter. Or there's something wrong with the printer and the ________________* (pl.) *are all printing ________________* (pl.). *It's probably my own fault for buying the cheapest word processor in town. My husband says it's a character ________________ of mine always insisting on buying cheap rubbish, but I can't help it if I've got Scottish ancestors, can I?*

---

word processor – Textverarbeitungsgerät

fertig sein

be ready? — **have finished?**

Ready and waiting

Mrs Wilson: *Well,* ***I'm ready****. I've been standing here with my hat and coat on for at least ten minutes.* ***Have you two finished*** *with what you were doing?*
Sally: *Just a second, Mum;* ***I've nearly finished****. I'm just sewing a button on my blouse. It came off just as I was putting it on.*
Mr Wilson: ***I haven't quite finished****. I'm just filling in these football pools. Surely it's worth waiting five minutes for a million pounds!*
Mrs Wilson: *Honestly,* ***you two are never ready*** *on time.*
Sally: *Oh, Mum, there's no great rush. Anyway, I think* ***we're all ready to go*** *now. Let's see if we're luckier at bingo than Dad has been with the pools for the last fifteen years.*

(football) pools – (etwa) (Fußball-)Toto ***bingo*** – Zahlenlotto

Die arme Mrs Wilson ist wieder mal ganz fix und fertig nach all der Warterei. Hoffentlich macht Sie dieses Stichwort nicht so schnell fertig. Sind Sie bereit für eine Aufklärung?

be ready

bereit sein, um etwas zu tun/unternehmen
I've got my case packed, so I'm ready.

Sehr oft in der Konstruktion:
be ready to do s.th.
be ready – bereit sein

have finished

(mit etwas) fertig sein, (etwas) beendet haben
I've spent all morning feeding this data into the computer. Thank goodness I've finished for today.

Sehr oft in der Konstruktion:
have finished (doing) s.th.

Übrigens: „mit etwas fertig sein" heißt auch ***be finished with s.th.***

be ready *oder* ***have finished?*** *Setzen Sie die passende Form ein.*

1. ______________ *you* ______________ *your lunch? I want to clear the table.*

2. ______________ *you* ______________ *to go now? If we don't leave very soon, we'll miss the train.*

3. *Please hand in the forms when you* ______________ *filling them in.*

4. *There are several patients in the waiting room, Dr Taylor.* ______________ *you* ______________ *to start surgery?*

---

surgery – Sprechstunde

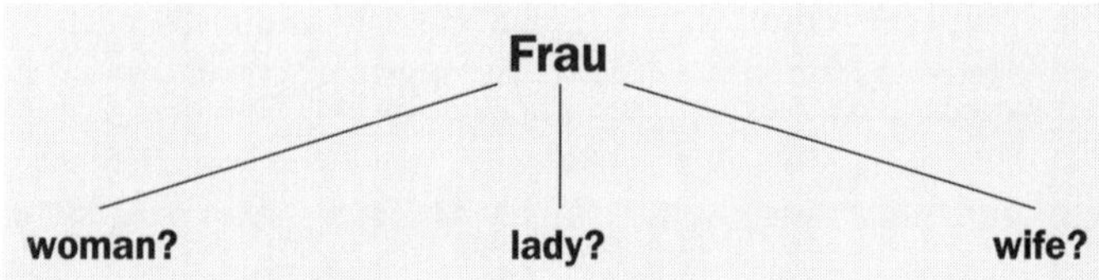

A real ladies' man

Henry the Eighth was fat, ugly, selfish and quite a hit with the ***ladies****. You could say he was a classic womanizer. In fact he liked* ***women*** *so much that he had six* ***wives****. Unfortunately for some of them, it was a case of fatal attraction.*

selfish – egozentrisch ***womanizer*** – Schürzenjäger ***fatal attraction*** – verhängnisvolle Anziehungskraft

woman

neutrale Bezeichnung für „Frau"; auch in Zusammensetzungen:
woman driver/teacher
Who says a woman's place is in the home?

⚠ Pluralform *women* (Aussprache [wimin])

lady

Dame, Frau, mit Betonung auf das Damenhafte; höfliche Bezeichnung für eine Frau
Who's that elegantly dressed lady over there?

wife

Ehefrau
He got quite a shock when all three of his ex-wives turned up at the party.

Zur Erinnerung noch: *man* – Mann, *husband* – Ehemann

Und wo wir beim Thema sind:
women's lib – die Frauenemanzipation

Und noch ein Tipp: Wenn Sie einen Brief an eine Frau adressieren, ist heute die moderne Form ***Ms*** (statt ***Miss***) bzw. ***Mrs*** (nur bei verheirateten Frauen).

woman, lady *oder* ***wife?***

I know so many ________________ (pl.), *but not one of them is good enough to be my* ________________. *I'm looking for a really elegant* ________________ *– someone I can show off to my friends. She doesn't have to be a very intelligent* ________________, *but I wouldn't object if she was rich.*

Fremder

stranger? **foreigner?**

Culture shock

Sally: *I've no idea where to start looking for the shop you want, Helmut. I'm a complete* ***stranger*** *here. Although I've lived in London all my life, I've never been to Willesden before.*
Helmut: *Well, it's no good asking anyone here. They're all* ***foreigners****.*
Sally: *What do you mean, Helmut? You may well be the only* ***foreigner*** *around here. These people are probably all British.*
Helmut: *But everyone looks foreign.*
Sally: *You can't go by the colour of people's skin, you know. It may seem strange to you, but you'll have to get used to the idea that Britain is very much a multiracial society. I'll have to take you to the Notting Hill Carnival in August and you can see for yourself – it's just like being in the Caribbean. And you'll find the only* ***foreigners*** *there will be tourists.*

stranger

1. Unbekannter
   The mountain tribes are still very suspicious of strangers.
2. ***I'm a stranger here.*** – Ich bin hier fremd.
   I'm a stranger here myself. This is the first time I've been to Oxford.

foreigner

Ausländer
Foreigners can have a hard time over here. They find very few English people who speak a foreign language.

Übrigens:
„Fremden …" in Zusammensetzungen wird oft mit ***tourist*** übersetzt:
tourist guide
tourist information centre
the tourist industry

stranger *oder* ***foreigner?***

1. *Who's that ______________ over there? I've never seen him at one of Sarah's parties before.*

2. *You used to be able to recognize ______________* (pl.) *by the way they dressed, but fashion has become so international that it's difficult to tell which country people come from these days.*

3. *Mothers should keep reminding their children not to speak to ______________* (pl.).

Freund(in)

friend? **boyfriend/girlfriend?**

Helmut the heartthrob

*Sally's **a good friend of mine** – we've known each other for years. But she's not **my girlfriend**. The way she talks to me sometimes, though, you might think she was my wife. Sally's got a **boyfriend** already, you see. Not that I mind. I have so many girls falling for me over here, I could have a different **girlfriend** every week. But I'm not like that. Actually, I quite fancy **one of Sally's friends** – Helen's her name, I think. She has such a lovely Scottish accent. I wonder if she's doing anything tonight ...*

heartthrob – Schwarm aller Mädchen ***fall for*** – sich verlieben in ***fancy*** – ganz gern mögen

Ein bisschen eingebildet ist der Helmut schon, oder? Freundlicherweise hat er uns aber den Unterschied zwischen den verschiedenen Arten von Freund(inn)en anschaulich vor Augen geführt.

friend

Freund, gute(r) Bekannte(r)
He doesn't seem to have many friends.
My friend Tom's coming to see us tomorrow.

boyfriend

Freund, mit dem man „geht"

girlfriend

Freundin, mit der man „geht"
Are she and her boyfriend ever going to get married?

"Has Judith got a new ________________?"
"Yes, he's called Terry. He's a ________________ from university. I can remember him – he used to spend all his time swotting in the library and wasn't at all interested in having a steady ________________ then."

---

swot – pauken, büffeln ***steady*** – fest

früher

... used to? **in the past?**

Poor Sally!

Sally: ***I used to go out*** *in the evenings a lot more, but these days I'm always so shattered when I get back from the office. We're definitely overworked and underpaid in our company.*
Helmut: *Well, in former times* ☹ *things were a lot worse.*
Sally: *In former times? You sound as if you're talking about the Middle Ages! And anyway, nobody uses that expression in everyday conversation. When we're talking about the past, we simply say* ***in the past****.*
Helmut: *Thank you, Sally. I was going to say that* ***in the past*** *people had a much harder time – they* ***used to work*** *far longer hours for less money.*
Sally: *Yes, I suppose we are better off these days, really. Anyway, shall we go down to the pub? I think I might just manage that. And I really fancy a drink.*
Helmut: *You know, you never* ***used to drink*** *so much, Sally.*
Sally: *It's a sign of overwork. And your bad influence.*

---

shattered – erschöpft, fertig, „kaputt" ***we are better off*** – es geht uns schon besser
fancy – Lust haben auf

used to

die geläufigste Übersetzung von „früher“ wird mit einer ***used to***-Konstruktion gebildet; dabei steht die (längst nicht mehr ausgeführte) Tätigkeit im Vordergrund

I used to be a racing driver.
Ich war früher Rennfahrer.

Did you really use to smoke?
Hast du früher wirklich geraucht?

in the past

wird für die weiter zurückliegende Vergangenheit verwendet (auch in Verbindung mit ***used to***); die zeitliche/geschichtliche Komponente steht im Vordergrund
People managed / used to manage without cars and television in the past.
In the past they used to put people like you in prison.

⚠ Der Ausdruck *in former times* ist im Englischen relativ selten anzutreffen. Er ist ein gehobener Ausdruck und bedeutet im historischen Kontext „in der Vergangenheit“ / „in früheren Zeiten“.

*Übersetzen Sie mit **used to** oder **in the past:***

1. *Früher hatten wir drei Hunde.*

2. *Du warst früher nicht so lustig.*

3. *Früher gab es in Europa viel mehr Monarchien.*

Garderobe

cloakroom? **hallstand?** **dressing-room?** **wardrobe?**

Behind the scenes

Sally: *I'd better take my coat – it's quite cold. Can you get it for me, Helmut? It's on the* ***hallstand****. We can leave our coats in the* ***cloakroom*** *at the theatre if we don't arrive late like the last time.*
Helmut: *Is this your coat? It looks new. You seem to have a large* ***wardrobe****.*
Sally: *How do you know, Helmut? You haven't seen my new bedroom yet.*
Helmut: *But I see you wearing a different outfit almost every day.*
Sally: *Oh, you mean I've got a lot of clothes! Yes, I suppose I have. You make me sound like Lady Di when you refer to my clothes as my* ***wardrobe****. Right then, Milord, off we go – the chauffeur will be waiting!*
Helmut: *Perhaps after the show we could go and see your cousin in her* ***dressing-room****. I've never been backstage before. And she does look very attractive in that photo you showed me …*

---

behind the scenes – hinter den Kulissen

cloakroom

Garderobenraum/Kleiderablage im Theater, Restaurant, Museum usw.
After the concert we had to queue up at the cloakroom for ten minutes to get our coats.

hallstand

Garderobe als Möbelstück
Most English homes have a hallstand in the hall.
Übrigens: ***coat rack*** – Garderobenhaken

dressing-room

Künstlergarderobe
Fans crowded into the star's dressing-room to congratulate her on her performance.

wardrobe

1. Kleiderschrank
   There's a big built-in wardrobe in the bedroom for all your clothes.
2. (gehoben) Kleiderbestand, Garderobe
   Politicians' wives are expected to have an extensive wardrobe while their husbands seem to walk around in the same old suits.

cloakroom, hallstand oder ***dressing-room?***

1. *We've got so many people coming this evening, we'll have to put their coats in the spare room. There won't be enough room on the ________________ .*

2. *I really object to having to pay to leave my coat in the ________________ at the Philharmonic. It ought to be free.*

3. *A lot of actors are quite superstitious. They always insist on having the same ________________, believing it will bring them luck.*

---

spare room – Gästezimmer ***superstitious*** – abergläubisch

glücklich

happy? **lucky?**

Don't worry, be happy

Jane: *You look very pleased with yourself.*
Clare: *Yes, I'm so* ***happy****. Do you remember that job I applied for? Well, there were at least sixty applicants, so I counted myself very* ***lucky*** *to be shortlisted. And then I actually got it!*
Jane: *Well, I've always said you were born under a lucky star – everything seems to fall right into your lap. Anyway, I'm very* ***happy*** *for you. Since your new job will mean a big increase in salary, I wonder if you could lend me some money?*
Clare: *You'll be lucky! I'm completely broke at the moment.*

---

applicant – Bewerber ***count o.s. lucky*** – sich glücklich schätzen ***be shortlisted*** – in die engere Wahl kommen ***lucky star*** – Glücksstern ***lap*** – Schoß ***You'll be lucky!*** – Keine Chance! ***broke*** – pleite

happy

(innerlich) glücklich
He doesn't look very happy about his pay rise.
Those were the happiest years of our lives.

be lucky

Glück/„Schwein" haben, sich glücklich schätzen können
Considering she had only had four driving lessons, she was lucky to have passed her test.

Übrigens:
lucky heißt sehr oft „Glücks …":
lucky star, lucky day, lucky number, lucky charm (= Glücksbringer)

happy oder **lucky?**

1. *Humphrey is sixty-five next year. He's not at all ______________ about having to retire, although he's ______________ he can stay on till then. Others have to take early retirement when they're sixty or younger.*

2. *He's just made a fortune on the stock market, ______________ old devil. But whether it'll make him ______________ is another matter.*

3. *You're very ______________ to have such an understanding wife.*

---

take early retirement – in den Vorruhestand treten ***stock market*** – Börse

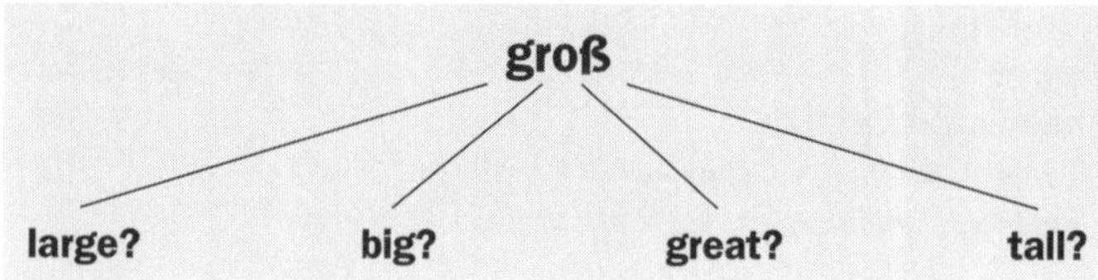

Home sweet home

Mrs Wilson: *This advertisement sounds quite interesting – DETACHED FIVE-BEDROOMED VICTORIAN HOUSE WITH* ***LARGE*** *GARDENS AT THE REAR.*
Peter: *Oh yes, I've always wanted a* ***lovely big*** *garden. It sounds great. I bet it's really expensive, though.*
Mrs Wilson: *Yes, it's only meant for the rich and* ***the great*** *with their* ***big*** *bank accounts, I'm afraid. I think we'll have to forget any* ***great*** *plans for a* ***large*** *country house surrounded by* ***tall*** *trees and acres of land ...*
Peter: *Just you wait. When I'm famous we'll have a* ***great big*** *mansion with a Rolls-Royce in front of the door, and stables with race horses, and ...*
Mrs Wilson: *That's* ***big*** *talk coming from someone who may well be on the dole one day.*

detached – frei stehend ***at the rear*** – hinten ***be on the dole*** – stempeln gehen

large

neutral-sachlich und etwas gehobener als *big* (vgl. hierzu auch *small* unter dem Stichwort **klein**)
This T-shirt's too small – I probably need a large size.

big

leicht umgangssprachlich und gefühlsbetont (vgl. auch *little* unter dem Stichwort **klein**); oft steht es nach einem anderen, gefühlsbetonten Adjektiv:
a nice big hamburger, a lovely big bathroom

great

1. (gehoben) sehr groß
   a great crowd of people
   (klingt beeindruckender als *a large crowd*)
2. groß(artig); bezieht sich auf eine Person, die etwas Großes geleistet hat oder auf eine hervorragende Leistung usw.
   a great man ist also ein Mann mit großen Verdiensten, seine Körpergröße spielt hier keine Rolle:
   Napoleon may not have been a big man, but for many he was a great statesman.
3. groß in Verbindung mit abstrakten Begriffen
   That was a great help.

Übrigens:
great big – (umgs.) eine feste Fügung, in der *big* durch Voransetzung von *great* positiv oder negativ verstärkt wird
You great big idiot!
He drives around in a great big limousine.

tall

groß im Sinne von hochgeschossen
a tall girl/tree/building/chimney usw.
(Hierfür kann auch *big* verwendet werden, wenn es eindeutig ist, dass es um die Höhe und nicht um den generellen Umfang geht.)

large, big, great *oder* ***tall?***

1. *The girls were so hungry after their swim that they bought themselves a great ________________ bag of chips each.*

2. *When ________________ money transfers are being handled, ________________ care must be taken to enter the correct account numbers.*

3. *You used to have to be quite ________________ to join the police force. Now height doesn't seem to matter.*

Haare

hair? **hairs?**

What lovely hair he's got.

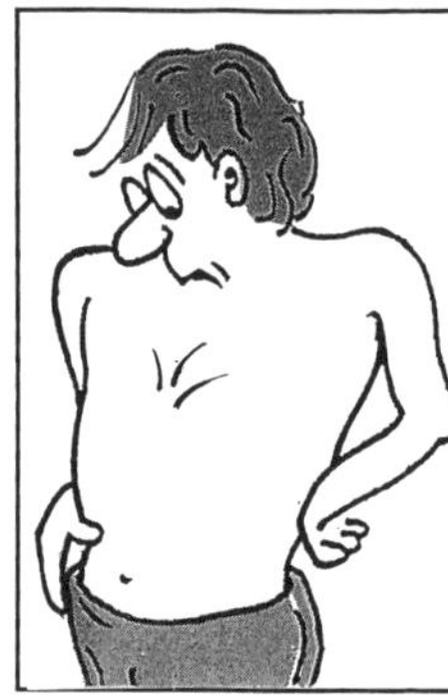

Still only five hairs?

Sie haben bestimmt nicht geahnt, mit was für einem haarigen Problem wir es hier zu tun haben. Deswegen brauchen Sie sich aber keine grauen Haare wachsen zu lassen: Es wird ja alles bis ins Einzelne – doch ohne Haarspalterei – erklärt:

hair

die Kopfhaare als Ganzes gesehen
You've got such nice blonde hair, I don't know why you had it cut so short.

hairs

sonstige Haare am Körper (auf der Brust, im Gesicht, an den Beinen usw.), besonders wenn man sie sich <u>einzeln</u> vorstellt; auch <u>einzelne</u> Kopfhaare
She was busy plucking some hairs from between her eyebrows.

hair kann hier benutzt werden, wenn man sich die Masse vorstellt bzw. wenn man höflich sein will:
facial hair, unwanted hair, chest hair
Have you ever tried wax to get rid of the hair on your legs?

Bei einem Satz wie *She washed her hairs* ☹ würde man sich vorstellen, dass sie sich ihre Haare einzeln gewaschen hat.

hair *oder* ***hairs?***

1. *I wish you wouldn't comb your ______________ at the table – we don't want ______________ in our cornflakes.*
2. *I can't even remember what colour ______________ he's got.*
3. *Did you know you're getting a few grey ______________?*

hören

listen (to)? — **hear?**

Mr Wilson loves ***listening to*** *Liszt's piano concertos.*

His neighbour can ***hear*** *the music loud and clear, too.*

listen (to)

aufmerksam/bewusst zuhören

I love listening to Liszt.

hear

passiv (mit)hören

I can hear your heart beating.

listen (to) *oder* ***hear?*** *Setzen Sie die passende Form ein.*

"_________________! Did you _________________ that noise? It sounded like the back door. Maybe it's a burglar, or a murderer!"
"I didn't _________________ a thing just now – you must be imagining things."
"Somebody was murdered in Hampstead last week, you know."
"Look, just go to sleep now, will you? I'm trying to _________________ the late-night news, and I don't want to _________________ another word about murderers in London."

kennen lernen

meet? — **get to know?**

Helmut falls head over heels

Sally: *Are you telling me you* ***met*** *this girl at the disco last night and you've decided to marry her?*
Helmut: *Yes. The moment I looked into her eyes, I knew this was the right woman for me …*
Sally: *But don't you think you should* ***get to know*** *her a bit better first, and perhaps* ***meet*** *her parents before you take such a big step?*
Helmut: *It was love at first sight …*

Sally: *Yes, I can see that. I don't think I've ever* ***met*** *anyone who falls in love as often as you do. Anyway, I'm off to see "Kramer vs. Kramer" again; perhaps you ought to come along too – you might learn something…*

---

fall head over heels (in love) – sich über beide Ohren verlieben

Und wir wollen jetzt diese zwei Ausdrücke ein bisschen näher kennen lernen:

meet s.o.

jdm. (das erste Mal) begegnen
I met him at an art exhibition.

get to know s.o.

jd. über einen Zeitraum näher/besser kennen lernen
It always takes me a few weeks to get to know my new pupils.

Das kurze ***meet*** bezieht sich auf eine kurze Begegnung zu irgendeinem Zeitpunkt.
Der längere Ausdruck ***get to know*** betont den längeren Vorgang des besseren Kennenlernens.

meet *oder* ***get to know?*** *Setzen Sie die passende Form ein.*

I first ______________ Roger in prison. As we both had to do five years, we had plenty of time to ______________ each other before deciding to go into business together.

klein

small? **little?**

Small is beautiful

Danny: *This is a photograph of my family taken about twenty years ago – we were quite a large family, as you can see. I was the eldest of six children, and we lived in this rather **small** cottage on the edge of a **romantic little village** in Dorset. This is Julie – she's the youngest. She was **small** and fat then, and really hates this photo.*
Pauline: *Oh, but she looks a **sweet little girl**. You were lucky to have such a big family – I was an only child. I would love to have had a **little sister**. And the cottage may have been **small**, but it looks a **lovely little place**. Much nicer than the tower blocks so many large families have to live in these days.*

only child – Einzelkind ***tower block*** – (großes) Hochhaus

small

neutral-sachlich (vgl. dazu auch *large* unter dem Stichwort **groß**)
I would prefer the smaller TV.

little

umgangssprachlicher als *small* und gefühlsbetont (vgl. auch *big* unter dem Stichwort **groß**); oft erscheint es nach einem anderen Adjektiv, das hierdurch betont wird:
a nasty little boy, a useful little book
(*small* wäre hier falsch)
my little sister – meine kleine (= jüngere) Schwester

little hat auch die Funktion der Endung „-chen" im Deutschen: „ein Häuschen" – *a little house*

small oder **little?**

1. *A sweet ______________ old lady paid my fare on the bus when I realized I'd left my purse at home.*
2. *It's much cheaper to buy the large economy packs of washing powder than the ______________ ones.*
3. *Before you sign that insurance form, you'd better have a good look at the ______________ print.*
4. *I had lovely curly hair when I was a ______________ girl.*

---

economy pack – Sparpackung

kochen

boil? **cook?** **make?**

What's cooking?

Peter: *Shall I* ***cook the dinner*** *for us tonight?*
Sally: *You* ***cook the dinner****? You can't even* ***boil an egg*** *properly.*
Peter: *And you sometimes make my blood boil with your sarcasm, Sally.*
Sally: *Sorry, Pete. Tell you what, why don't you* ***make some coffee*** *while Helmut and I get on with the serious business of* ***making dinner****? It's your favourite – rump steak with* ***boiled potatoes*** *and mushrooms.*
Peter: *Okay, chef, here's some strong coffee coming up …*

---

make s.o.'s blood boil – jd. rasend machen

boil

1. (in Wasser, Milch usw.) kochen, im Gegensatz zu braten usw.; betont die Art der Zubereitung
   You boil potatoes/vegetables/rice/an egg.
2. kochen (Wasser, Milch usw.)
   The water's boiling – shall I put the spaghetti in?

cook

1. (Gemüse, Fleisch usw.) zubereiten, kochen, im Gegensatz zu nicht kochen; die Art des Zubereitens wird nicht genannt
   How should I cook this meat/these vegetables?
2. (ein Gericht, das Essen) zubereiten
   When you're single, it doesn't seem worth cooking a meal every evening.
3. kochen; das Essen machen
   I've taught my husband to enjoy cooking.

make

1. (ein Gericht, das Essen) zubereiten
   make (the) dinner – das Essen kochen
   How do you make Tandoori chicken?
2. (Kaffee, Tee) kochen
   Who made this tea? It's far too weak.

boil, cook *oder* ***make?*** *Setzen Sie die passende Form ein.*

1. *Should we have fried rice, or should we ________________ it and cut down on our calories?*

2. *I seem to have spent the whole day ________________ tea for the workmen.*

3. *Who ________________ for you while you were ill?*

---

workmen – Handwerker

kontrollieren

check? **control?**

Better late than never

My last trip to London by plane was a nightmare. We spent over an hour having our passports ***checked*** *and luggage inspected at Passport and Customs Control. Then on the plane the steward had to* ***check*** *all our tickets as there was one passenger too many. To top it all, the pilot announced that the air-traffic controllers hadn't given permission to take off as mechanics had to* ***check*** *the instruments for a technical fault. Just as I was finding it difficult to* ***control*** *myself any longer, the pilot assured us that everything was under control and we would arrive in London with only three hours' delay.*

to top it all – um das Maß voll zu machen ***delay*** – Verspätung

check

(Papiere, Fahrkarten, Instrumente usw.) nachprüfen; nachsehen
Did you remember to check the oil level?

Denken Sie an die Checkliste und das Einchecken.

control

unter Kontrolle halten/haben, steuern, regeln
Why is it that some countries can control inflation and others can't?

Und nun, wie immer, die kleine Selbstkontrolle. Sie dürfen überprüfen, ob Sie auch alles „gecheckt“ haben:

***check** oder **control?** Setzen Sie die passende Form ein.*

1. *After a thorough medical checkup, the doctor recommended Jim to ______________ his weight regularly and try to ______________ it by strict dieting.*
2. *House prices are skyrocketing. I wish the government would do something to ______________ them.*
3. *All bags had to be ______________ by security men before visitors were allowed into the museum.*
4. *The ticket inspectors are after those fare dodgers – I had my ticket ______________ three times today.*

---

skyrocket – in die Höhe schnellen ***fare dodger*** – Schwarzfahrer

krank

ill? **sick?**

It's enough to make you sick

Helmut: *You're back early from the office, Sally. Is anything wrong?*
Sally: *It's a virus. I **feel** quite **ill**.*
Helmut: *You do **look ill**. What sort of virus is it?*
Sally: *A computer virus. It's ruined six weeks of work on our latest project.*
Helmut: *That's terrible!*

Sally: *Yes, I think I'll crawl into bed and try to forget all about it. I'll get the doctor to give me a* ***sick note****.*
Helmut: *It must have given you a bit of a shock – you've gone quite green.*
Sally: *Yes, in fact I think I'm going to be sick …*
Helmut: *Hang on! I'll get you a bucket!*

ill

krank; meist mit einem Verb und fast nie vor einem Substantiv
feel ill, be ill, look ill, fall ill
If you're so ill, you won't be able to go to Kim's party tonight either.

sick

⚠ Beachten Sie die unterschiedlichen Bedeutungen:

1. krank, Krank(en) …; meist vor einem Substantiv
   a sick child
   a sick note
   sick pay, sick leave
2. ***I feel sick.*** – Mir ist übel/schlecht.
   I'm going to be sick. – Ich muss mich übergeben.
3. besonders amerikanisch für *ill*
   He's very sick. They're going to operate on him next week.

---

sick leave – Krankenurlaub

✎ ***ill*** oder ***sick?***

1. *She's critically ____________ and has been put into the intensive care unit.*
2. *I hate crossing the Channel by ferry – I always feel ____________, even when the sea isn't rough.*
3. *One of our senior executives was suddenly taken ____________ during a board meeting. He's such a workaholic, I'm not at all surprised.*
4. *When I smell fish frying, I always feel I want to be____________.*

---

senior executive – leitender Manager ***board meeting*** – Vorstandssitzung

Kritik

criticism? **review?**

Criticising the critic

Glenda: *He can't take* ***criticism*** *from anyone – especially if you say something negative about the way he dresses. But when he writes his* ***theatre reviews*** *for the paper, he never has a good word for anyone. You'd think all his negative remarks and* ***criticisms*** *would get on the readers' nerves, not to mention the poor actors and directors who get all those bad write-ups. You should have read his devastating* ***review*** *of "Hamlet" and my performance of Ophelia!*
Lawrence: *Well, if you feel so strongly about it, perhaps you should write to the papers. But don't be too critical – you know how easily your father gets offended.*

director – Regisseur ***devastating*** – vernichtend ***if you feel so strongly about it*** – wenn es dir so sehr am Herzen liegt ***get offended*** – beleidigt werden

Und jetzt wird's wieder kritisch:

criticism

1. bestimmte, konkrete Kritik
   That's a very fair criticism.
2. das Kritisieren, Kritisiererei
   All you ever hear from her is criticism.

review

(auch ***write-up***) Rezension
Their new CD got some very good reviews.

critic

1. (auch ***reviewer***) Rezensent
   He wants to be a theatre critic for one of the Sunday papers.
2. Kritiker
   She's a severe critic of commercial TV.

criticism *oder* ***review?***

"I can't stand your ______________ any more. You've complained about every single one of my novels so far."
"Well, I'm only repeating what the critics say in their ____________ (pl.)."

Kurve

bend? **corner?** **curve?**

Helmut: *Be careful, Sally! There's another one of those hairpin curves.* ☹

Sally: *You mean* ***hairpin bends****, Helmut; and anyway I'm used to these winding roads. You concentrate on your English and I'll worry about the driving. In geometry you can talk about a* ***curve****, but when we're driving we use the word* ***bend*** *or* ***corner****.*

Helmut: *Sally, watch out! Don't cut the bends* ☹ *like that!*

Sally: *Sorry, Helmut, it's* ***cut the corners****. I'm keeping as close to the side as I can. Anyway, the only* ***curves*** *I thought you'd be interested in are Marilyn Monroe's.*

Helmut: *Marilyn Monroe's?*

Sally: *Well, I thought she was supposed to have been the actress with the most* ***shapely curves*** *in Hollywood.*

Helmut: *Sometimes the English language just drives me round the bend!*

---

tough going – schwieriges Vorankommen ***shapely*** – wohl geformt

Ja, beim letzten Satz hat er es richtig getroffen, und Recht hat er noch dazu: Die Feinheiten der englischen Sprache sind manchmal schon zum Verrücktwerden – *they drive you round the bend.* Aber ein bisschen Übung und Helmut kriegt bestimmt noch die Kurve. Sie hoffentlich auch!

bend

Kurve einer Straße
The bends in this road are making me feel sick.

corner

Straßenkurve in bestimmten festen Fügungen
cut the corner – die Kurve schneiden
take the corner too fast – zu schnell in die Kurve gehen
Und im übertragenen Sinn:
try to cut corners – den schnellen Weg suchen
You can't cut corners learning English. – Beim Englischlernen gibt es keine bequemen Wege.

curve

1. geometrische/grafische Kurve; Bogen, Kurvenverlauf
   The curve on the graph showed a slight increase in sales.
   The coastline stretched away in a gentle curve.
2. (pl., humorvoll) die körperlichen Rundungen
   She was wearing a dress that hugged her curves.

bend, corner *oder* ***curve?***

1. *Careful when you're driving – that road is full of sharp* ________________ (pl.).

2. *This is supposed to be a straight line, not a* ________________.

3. *I wish the students would keep to the footpath instead of always cutting the* ________________ (pl.).

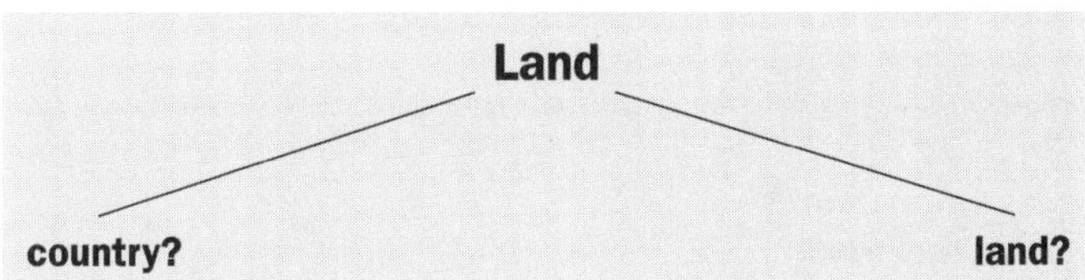

Going to the dogs

What is this ***country*** *coming to? We used to think it was wonderful – people would call it a* ***land of plenty****, the* ***land of the free*** *and so on. But when you look at the dreadful economic situation, the unemployment and crime rates, and the growing gap between rich and poor, it makes you want to emigrate. Yes, I think that's what I'll do – I'll move to a sunnier climate, buy myself a little plot of* ***land*** *out in the* ***country*** *somewhere and cultivate my garden. And maybe when I'm old and grey I'll come back and visit the* ***country*** *I grew up in to see whether anything has improved …*

---

be going to the dogs – vor die Hunde gehen

country

1. Land im geographischen Sinn
   The package tour was good value for money – we saw five countries in two weeks.
2. Land im Gegensatz zu Stadt
   life in the country – das Leben auf dem Land

land

1. literarische bzw. emotionale Bezeichnung für „Land"/„Nation"; oft in einer festen Fügung
   a land of milk and honey
   He told us of faraway lands and exotic cities.
2. Grund(besitz)
   All this land, as far as the eye can see, belongs to me.
   plot/piece of land – Grundstück
3. Festland; Land im Gegensatz zum Meer
   After being on the raft for a week, the refugees finally sighted land.

---

package tour – Pauschalreise ***good value for money*** – sehr preiswert, sein Geld wert

country *oder* ***land?***

1. *If you could choose, which ____________ would you like to live in?*

2. *Japan is known as the "____________ of the Rising Sun", though some people used to call it the "____________ of the Rising Yen".*

3. *He's always boasting about how many different ____________* (pl.) *he's visited.*

4. *You have to be rich to buy ____________ in this ____________, or else marry one of the royals.*

Landschaft

countryside? **scenery?** **landscape?**

Slow progress

Mrs Wilson: *You see so much more when you travel by train. The* ***countryside*** *around here is just beautiful.*
Mr Wilson: *Yes, we've seen some* ***lovely scenery****. It makes a change from the* ***bleak landscapes*** *we saw up in Iceland last summer.*
Mrs Wilson: *I've always dreamed of a holiday in Ireland, and here we are, surrounded by all this wonderful* ***green countryside****…*
Mr Wilson: *Yes, here we are, stuck in the middle of nowhere, not knowing whether the train's broken down or the driver's gone off to the nearest pub for a drink.*
Mrs Wilson: *As I was saying, you see a lot more of the* ***countryside*** *from a train…*

---

bleak – trostlos, trist

countryside

betont das Erlebnis der Landschaft als Ganzes und oft den anmutigen Charakter; für den Engländer heißt *countryside* vorwiegend sattes Grün, sanfte Hügel und Felder usw.
A few weeks in the Devon countryside will do you the world of good.

scenery

Landschaft mit Betonung auf deren (beeindruckender) Schönheit; Landschaft, wie sie an einem (z. B. beim Zugfahren) vorbeizieht
We saw so much spectacular scenery on our bicycle tour through New Zealand.

landscape

1. Landschaftsbild, Landschaft aus der Ferne betrachtet
   From the top of that hill you get a marvellous view of the whole landscape.
   a landscape – auch „Landschaftsbild“ in der Malerei
2. neutrale, fast wissenschaftliche Bezeichnung; betont den (geologischen) Charakter, die Konturen der Landschaft und wird oft mit flachen und/oder trostlosen Gegenden assoziiert
   The film is set in a flat, grey, windswept Siberian landscape.
   landscape architect/gardener/artist

   vgl. *moonscape* (Mondlandschaft)
   townscape (Stadtansicht)
   seascape (Meeresansicht/Seestück)

countryside, scenery *oder* ***landscape?***

1. *It's a volcanic ______________ with very unusual vegetation.*

2. *I'm really looking forward to our holiday in Ireland – all that lovely ______________ to go for long walks in.*

3. *We saw some marvellous ______________ driving along the Californian coast.*

lassen

let? — **leave?**

Leave it to me!

*Don't forget to **let** the cat out before you go to bed, but don't **leave** him out all night. And when you **let** him in, don't **leave** the door unlocked again. We don't want to **let** the burglars in as well.*

burglar – Einbrecher

let	leave
Let the water out.	*Leave the money here.*
(= run out)	(= where it is)
Let him in now.	*Leave him in the garden.*
(= come in)	(= where he is)
Der Zustand wird **geändert**.	Der Zustand **bleibt unverändert**.

66 ***let** oder **leave?** Setzen Sie die passende Form ein.*

1. *There have been so many bomb scares in Britain that people travelling are warned not to ____________ their luggage unattended.*
2. *Being a painter, I need a flat with large windows that ____________ in plenty of light.*
3. *Oliver was so afraid of the dark that he begged his mother to ____________ the light on in the hall.*
4. *Most European countries are trying to control the flood of immigrants and are refusing to ____________ many of them enter the country.*

bomb scare – Bombenwarnung ***unattended*** – unbeaufsichtigt

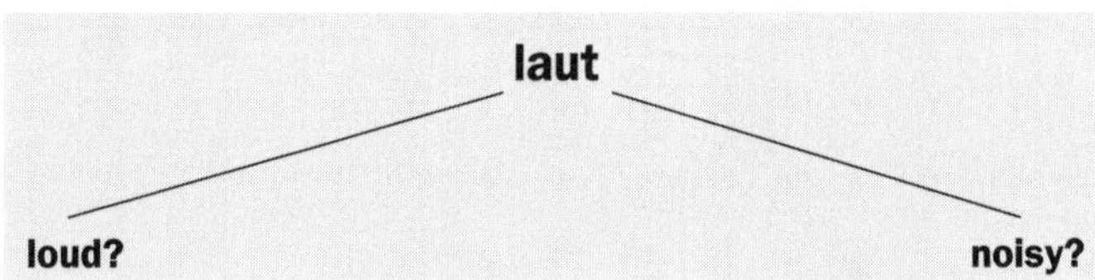

Noise pollution

Peter: *I can't hear you. What did you say?*
Mrs Wilson: *I wasn't speaking to you. I was muttering to myself. Anyway, that music's so* ***loud*** *it's impossible to hold a conversation here.*
Peter: *But it's heavy metal, Mum – it's got to be* ***loud****. You needn't worry about the people next door; they're very* ***noisy*** *themselves. You can often hear their* ***loud*** *voices and laughter quite late at night.*
Mrs Wilson: *Well, just because we have one lot of* ***noisy*** *neighbours, there's no need to deafen the whole street with our new stereo.*

noise pollution – „Lärmverschmutzung", Lärmbelästigung(en)

loud

laut vom Ton her (das Gegenteil wäre „leise"); beschreibt Dinge, die direkt mit einem Ton in Verbindung gesetzt werden (denken Sie an Lautstärke)
a loud voice/stereo/engine
loud music/laughter/clapping

Wird besonders auch für kurze Laute oder Geräusche verwendet:
a loud bang/scream/crash/noise

noisy

(anhaltend oder dauerhaft) lärmend, geräuschvoll (das Gegenteil wäre „ruhig"); bezieht sich eher auf die Geräuschkulisse und wird meist als unangenehm empfunden
a noisy place/restaurant/street/person/family/car
noisy children/traffic/aircraft
We've got very noisy neighbours. They stamp about like a herd of elephants.

loud *oder* ***noisy?***

1. *I work with ten other typists in an open-plan office. It's terribly ________________.*

2. *The ________________ music and the ________________ people were getting on my nerves, so I went home.*

3. *Do you have to turn the radio up so ________________?*

---

open-plan office – Großraumbüro

leicht

light? **slight?** **easy?**

Taking things lightly

Mrs Wilson: *I've got a* ***slight headache*** *and I feel a bit shivery. I think I'm coming down with something.*
Mr Wilson: *I'm not surprised. It was quite chilly yesterday and you were only wearing a* ***light summer dress****.*
Mrs Wilson: *Well, it's not so* ***easy to tell*** *what the weather's going to be like at this time of year.*
Mr Wilson: *That's true. Anyway, I don't suppose it's anything serious – you'll probably just get a* ***slight cold****. Next time wear something more suitable.*
Mrs Wilson: *That's* ***easier said than done****.*

---

take s.th. lightly – etwas auf die leichte Schulter nehmen ***be coming down with s.th.*** – etwas ausbrüten ***I feel shivery*** – mich fröstelt ***chilly*** – kühl ***suitable*** – passend

Gar nicht so leicht, oder? Aber um Ihnen die Arbeit ein wenig zu erleichtern, haben wir die Erklärungen möglichst leicht verdaulich gestaltet. Wohl bekomm's!

light

1. von geringem Gewicht
   That leather case is much too heavy for you to carry. Try this one – it's nice and light.
2. leicht verdaulich, auch im übertragenen Sinn anspruchslos, unterhaltsam
   light music/entertainment/reading
   In summer when it's hot I prefer a light lunch.
   I usually read a magazine in the evening – I like something light before I go to bed.

slight

geringfügig, unbedeutend
a slight headache/cold/pain/temperature/error
There has been a slight improvement in the patient's health.

easy

einfach, mühelos
A lot of men claim that housework has become very easy with all the modern household appliances. They should try it more often!

---

household appliance – Haushaltsgerät

light, slight oder ***easy?***

1. *Helmut's English is really very good. He's just got a ____________ German accent, but you hardly notice it.*
2. *You don't weigh much. You're as ____________ as a feather.*
3. *The plane had to make a forced landing, but fortunately no one was hurt and there was only ____________ damage to one of the wings.*
4. *It's relatively ____________ for young children to pick up a foreign language.*

leihen

borrow? **lend?**

Bringing up parents

*Why don't you **borrow** money **from** the bank, Dad, instead of always asking me to **lend you** some? And I wish you wouldn't keep taking my comics away – I told you I'll be glad to **lend them to you** if you ask me first.*

borrow s.th. from s.o.

– sich etwas von jdm. leihen
You borrow money from a bank.

lend s.o. s.th., lend s.th. (out) to s.o.

– jdm. etwas (aus)leihen; erscheint oft mit einem Possessivpronomen zusammen (*my, your* usw.)
I lent him my bike. / I lent my bike (out) to him.
My sister won't lend me the money.

Bei ***borrow*** bekommt man etwas, bei ***lend*** wird man etwas los.

borrow oder **lend?** Setzen Sie die passende Form ein.

"I ________________ Jenny's video recorder last night, but I've broken it. D'you think you could ________________ me yours?"
"You've got a nerve. The last time I ________________ something to you, I never got it back."
"What was it I ________________ from you, then?"
"My boyfriend!"

lernen

study? **revise?** **learn?**

Give me a break!

Mrs Wilson: *If you've got an English exam tomorrow, Helmut, I think you'd better stay in and* ***study for it*** *instead of going out with the girls again.*
Helmut: *But I've been* ***revising*** *all week, Mrs Wilson. I've* ***learnt my tenses*** *and I've* ***revised*** *nearly all* ***my*** *old* ***vocabulary****. I need to relax now, otherwise I'll be too nervous to concentrate tomorrow.*
Mrs Wilson: *The last time you went out the night before an English test, you were so relaxed we couldn't get you out of bed the next morning. I sincerely hope this isn't the way you* ***study for your exams*** *at university in Germany.*

Das will gelernt sein! Deswegen geht's mit dem Studieren gleich weiter:

study

betont die Lerntätigkeit / die geistige Auseinandersetzung zum besseren Verständnis
Why is it that the weather's always so nice when I have to stay inside and study?
study for an exam – für eine Prüfung lernen

revise

1. lernen durch Wiederholung
   He was up all night revising for his biology exams.
   Übrigens: ***swot (up)*** = pauken, büffeln
2. (Stoff) wiederholen
   I've still got to revise my lecture notes.

learn

(etwas) lernen; die Beherrschung des Lernstoffs steht im Vordergrund
learn a language
learn one's grammar/tenses/vocabulary
I spend so much time studying, yet I don't seem to be learning very much.

---

lecture – Vorlesung

study, revise *oder* ***learn?*** *Setzen Sie die passende Form ein.*

"You look tired – have you been locked away in your room ________________ again?"
"Yes, I've been ________________ all this term's history. I had to ________________ so many new dates for the test tomorrow, and ________________ all the old ones. But even though I know all these dates off by heart, I don't feel I've really ________________ very much about the subject."

term – Trimester ***know s.th. off by heart*** – etwas auswendig kennen/wissen

lustig sein

be fun? **be funny?**

Fun and games

I love going out with Derek – he's ***great fun****. He's got so many* ***funny jokes and stories*** *up his sleeve, he has you in fits of laughter. It can't be much* ***fun*** *for him being married to Dorothy, though. She's so serious and never seems to see the* ***funny side*** *of things. No wonder Derek's such a comedian – it's probably the only way he can stay sane.*

have s.th. up one's sleeve – etwas auf Lager haben ***fit of laughter*** – Lachanfall
stay sane – den Verstand bewahren, „normal" bleiben

it's fun

es macht Spaß, ist sehr unterhaltsam
It's no fun dining out with someone who's on a diet and is a teetotaller as well.

it's funny

es ist komisch/lustig, bringt einen zum Lachen
The clown was so funny, he even made all the grown-ups laugh.

teetotaller – Antialkoholiker

fun oder **funny?**

1. *I've never been able to appreciate slapstick comedy. What's so ______________ about someone slipping on a banana skin?*
2. *They call New York "Fun City", but it's not much ______________ if you're unemployed and have to sleep on a park bench at night.*
3. *For kids the circus is great ______________. They find everything the clowns do ______________, even the silliest things.*

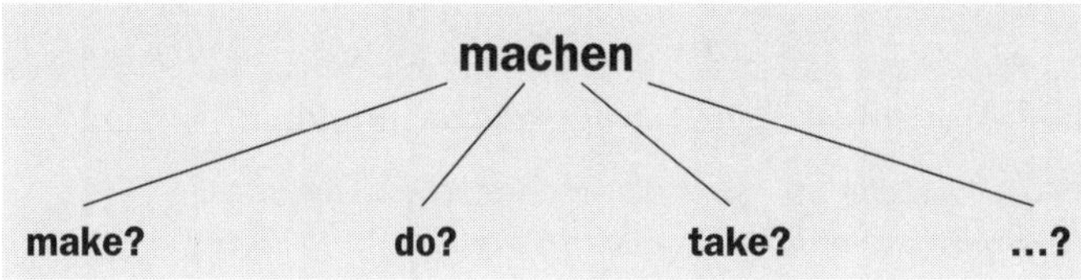

Making a mountain out of a molehill

Lucy: *I'm **doing** so much **overtime** at the moment, plus I'm **doing a** word-processing **course**, and I'm supposed to be **taking a test** next week.*
Anne: *Well, I think you **do** far too much. You're just **making life difficult** for yourself. Why don't you **have a break** and **take a trip** to the Mediterranean or somewhere?*
Lucy: *It's all right for you to **make suggestions** like that. You never seem to have any problem taking time off and **going on holiday**.*
Anne: *It's just a matter of **making the most of** life, that's all.*

---

make a mountain out of a molehill – aus einer Mücke einen Elefanten machen

Bevor wir Sie mit „machen" noch ganz fertig machen, bieten wir Ihnen lieber eine kleine Auswahl aus dem breit gefächerten Angebot an. Machen wir uns also ran an die Arbeit!

make

das <u>Endprodukt</u> steht im Vordergrund

1. etwas herstellen/produzieren
   make some tea / a cake / a mess / a noise usw.
   What are you making? – Was machst/bastelst/kochst du (da)?
2. im Abstrakten
   make progress – Fortschritte machen
   make a mistake – einen Fehler machen
   make a fuss – ein Theater machen

do

die Tätigkeit (das „Tun") steht im Vordergrund

do the washing up – den Abwasch machen, abspülen
do the/some shopping – Einkäufe machen
do one's room – sein Zimmer machen
do the housework – die Hausarbeiten machen
do one's homework – seine Hausaufgaben machen
do one's hair – sich die Haare machen
do/take a course – einen Kurs machen
do sports – Sport machen
do overtime – Überstunden machen
What are you doing? – Was machst/tust du (da)?

■ Feststehende Ausdrücke
take an exam / a test – eine Prüfung machen
take a photo – ein Foto machen
take / have a break – (eine) Pause machen
take a trip to … – eine Reise nach … machen

go on holiday – Urlaub machen
go on a trip to … – eine Reise nach … machen
go on a bicycle tour – eine Radtour machen
go for a walk – einen Spaziergang machen

⚠ ***have an unpleasant / a pleasant experience***
eine unangenehme/angenehme Erfahrung machen

Ergänzen Sie die fehlenden Wörter.

1. *You're ____________ so much noise in the kitchen – what on earth are you ____________?*

2. *I just don't find any time to ____________ the housework or to ____________ my English homework.*

3. *When my husband and I ____________ holiday we always like to ____________ something different. Last year we ____________ a bicycle tour; this year we're planning to ____________ a photography course in the South of France. I've never ____________ photographs before, so it should be fun.*

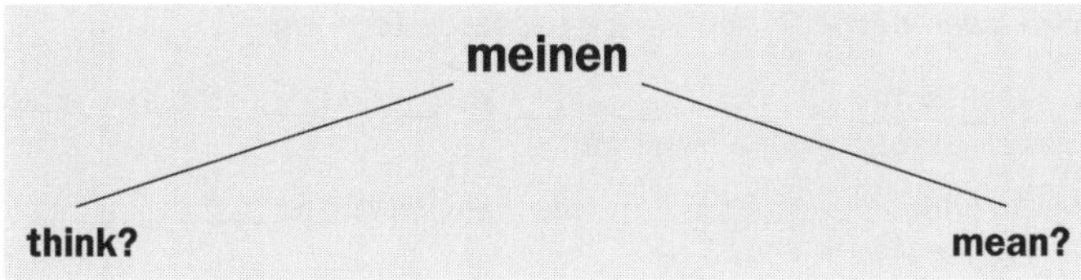

Eating out

Helmut: *See that man over there with the funny hairstyle?*
Sally: *Which one do you* ***mean*** *exactly?*
Helmut: *The one with the silly red bow tie, sitting in the corner. Don't you* ***think*** *he looks absolutely ridiculous? I'm surprised they let him into this restaurant.*
Sally: *Just a minute, I must put my glasses on ... Hey, that's Rodney!*
Helmut: *You don't* ***mean*** *Rodney your ex-boyfriend?*
Sally: *Yes, I do. Now, Helmut, would you mind briefly explaining exactly what you* ***mean*** *by "ridiculous" before I go over and join Rod? I* ***think*** *he must be feeling a bit lonely sitting over there all by himself ...*

bow tie – Fliege ***ridiculous*** – lächerlich

think

glauben, denken
I'm a firm believer in animal rights, but I think throwing paint at women in fur coats is going too far.

mean

1. (damit) sagen wollen
   What exactly do you mean by that?
2. sich beziehen auf, sprechen von
   I mean her, the woman in the fur coat.

think *oder* ***mean?*** *Setzen Sie die passende Form ein.*

1. *What do you ________________ – shall we eat first and then go to the cinema, or eat afterwards?*
2. *No, I don't ________________ the diamond ring, I ________________ the one with the five rubies – don't you ________________ it would suit me?*
3. *I also ________________ children ought to start learning a foreign language in kindergarten.*

merken

notice? — **realize?**

Developing in all directions

Mrs Wilson: *Do you* ***realize*** *how much weight you're putting on?*
Mr Wilson: *No, I hadn't* ***noticed****, actually.*
Mrs Wilson: *Well, I can see it a mile away. I think it's time you cut down on your drinking. We don't want anyone saying you've got a beer belly, do we now?*

Mr Wilson: *Do you **realize** you're beginning to sound more and more like my mother?*

cut down on – einschränken ***beer belly*** – Bierbauch

Mrs Wilson merkt aber auch alles. Und Sie haben hoffentlich den unterschiedlichen Gebrauch der zwei englischen Verben bemerkt:

notice

zufällig/nebenbei mit den Sinnen (Augen, Ohren usw.) wahrnehmen, merken
I hadn't noticed – es war mir nicht aufgefallen
Fortunately he didn't seem to notice the tomato ketchup on my tie.

realize

mit dem Verstand wahrnehmen, gewahr werden
I hadn't realized – es war mir nicht bewusst/klar
I didn't realize he had eaten all the salad up.

⚠ nicht mit *recognize* verwechseln (siehe dazu auch das Stichwort **erkennen**)

***notice** oder **realize?** Setzen Sie die passende Form ein.*

1. *"Did you ______________ how thin Jeremy looked at the wedding?" – "Yes, I did. I hardly recognized him."*
2. *She didn't ______________ that he was just after her money.*
3. *I had ______________ how expensive his clothes were, but I only ______________ how rich he was when I happened to read that he was one of the top ten earners in the country.*

top earner – Spitzenverdiener

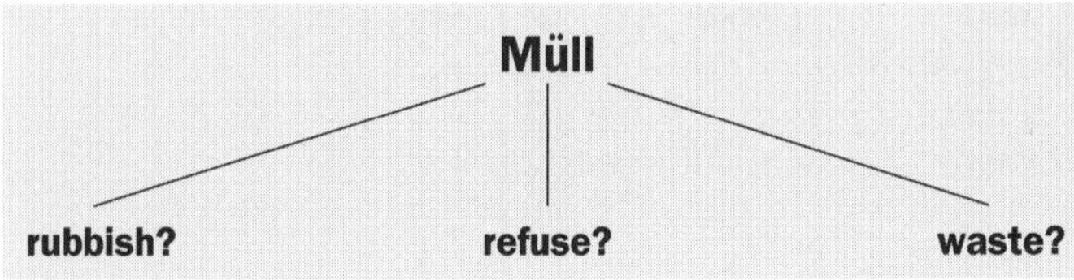

It's not a load of garbage

Helmut: *What shall I do with all this* ***rubbish****?*
Sally: *If the dustbin's full, put it in a plastic bag. The dustmen will be emptying the bins tomorrow anyway.*
Helmut: *Dustmen?*
Sally: *Yes. Or* ***refuse collectors****, if you prefer their official name.*
Helmut: *But what about these bottles? We shouldn't just throw them away.*
Sally: *Well, I'm afraid the nearest bottle bank is about a mile away. I'm usually too lazy to take them there.*
Helmut: *Well I'm not. I feel very strongly about it. In Germany lots of people separate their* ***waste*** *into three different bins – one for glass, one for waste paper, and a third for general* ***household rubbish****.*
Sally: *Yes, I suppose it's a good idea, really. I used to think environmentalists talked a lot of rubbish, but we do seem to be producing far too much* ***waste*** *in the home.*
Helmut: *It's not just* ***household refuse****. Just think of all the* ***industrial waste*** *that's polluting our rivers.*
Sally: *And the lakes and seas. You're right, Helmut. We're a bit behind over here when it comes to "green awareness". I'm not surprised that some people on the Continent still call us the dirty man of Europe!*

---

bottle bank – Altglascontainer ***green awareness*** – Umweltbewusstsein

rubbish

Müll, besonders Hausmüll, Abfälle
It's amazing how much rubbish even a single-person household can produce.
Am. und zunehmend auch Brit.: ***garbage, trash***

refuse

Müll, Abfall; amtliche/formelle Bezeichnung (Betonung auf der ersten Silbe!)
The local council is responsible for refuse collection and for providing public refuse tips.

waste

Müll mit Betonung auf die Masse; oft global gesehen und vor allem auch Industrie- und Sondermüll
household waste, industrial waste
chemical/toxic/hazardous/radioactive waste

Übrigens:
rubbish, garbage und ***trash*** bedeuten salopp im übertragenen Sinn auch „Quatsch"/„Unsinn"
Why do so many politicians talk rubbish on subjects they know nothing about?
litter – herumliegender Abfall auf der Straße, im Park usw.

---

local council – Gemeinde ***refuse tip*** – Müllabladeplatz

rubbish, refuse *oder* ***waste?***

1. *The factory was fined for pumping its ______________ into a nearby river.*
2. *Just look at all this ______________ in the streets. No wonder there are so many rats in this city.*
3. *Liverpool City Council has just opened three new ______________ tips.*

---

be fined – eine Geldstrafe zahlen müssen

nächste(r,-s)

nearest? **next?**

*Where's the **nearest** toilet?*

*Where's the **next** toilet?*

nearest

nächst**gelegen**e(r-,-s), meist vom Sprecher/Subjekt aus gesehen
We must get him to the nearest hospital fast.
(Es ist hier unmittelbar <u>kein</u> Krankenhaus.)

next

nächste(r,-s) **in einer Reihe**, räumlich oder zeitlich
This is only the fourth floor – he works on the next floor.
I've just missed my plane to Mombasa – when's the next flight?

Noch ein Beispiel:
We took him to the <u>nearest</u> hospital, but they didn't have the necessary medical equipment, so he was rushed to the <u>next</u> hospital.

Gelegentlich, im amerikanischen Englisch sogar häufig, wird *next* in der Bedeutung von *nearest* gebraucht.

nearest *oder* ***next?***

I was crawling through the desert dying of thirst and had collapsed under an acacia tree. When a bedouin came riding along on his camel I asked him where the ______________ oasis was. He told me to turn sharp right at the ______________ acacia tree and carry on for two miles. When I finally got to the oasis, there was a sign up saying "Sorry, no beer". So I had a sip of water and set off for the ______________ oasis, hoping to get there before the bar closed.

in der Nähe (von)

near? **nearby?**

It's a dog's life

Man in park: *I've seen you in this park with your Rottweilers quite often. Do you live* ***nearby****?*
Dog owner: *No, I live on the other side of town,* ***near St John's Hospital****. But every time the dogs foul the paths or the grass in the* ***nearby park****, somebody reports me and I get fined. So we come here instead. People are much more tolerant here than in our part of town.*
Man in park: *That's what you think. I live quite* ***near here****, and I've been watching you and your dogs. You should be hearing from the Department of the Environment very soon …*

---

foul – verunreinigen ***get/be fined*** – eine Geldstrafe zahlen müssen ***Department of the Environment*** – Umweltministerium

near

in der Nähe <u>von</u> ...
near the shops, near my school

nearby

1. in der/dessen/deren Nähe; steht oft am Satzende und bezieht sich auf einen <u>schon genannten</u> Ort
   We live in Richmond Road, and Dave's parents live in the council flats nearby.
2. nahe (gelegen); steht <u>vor</u> einem Substantiv
   They had to tow the car to <u>a</u> nearby garage.
   We get a lot of noise from <u>the</u> nearby football stadium.

In dieser Bedeutung steht der Artikel *(a/the)* immer <u>vor</u> *nearby*:
<u>a</u> nearby hospital
<u>the</u> nearby airport

Ein beliebter Fehler, den Sie auf jeden Fall vermeiden sollten, ist zu sagen *nearby the ...* ☹
Richtig heißt es: *near the ...*

Übrigens:
„in der Nähe" wird auch oft übersetzt als *near there, not far away, in the vicinity/area*

---

council flats – (etwa) Sozialwohnungen ***tow*** – abschleppen

near *oder* ***nearby?***

George's new company is on the other side of the river, ________ the race track. We're hoping to find a suitable house ________, although I haven't seen a supermarket anywhere ________ there. The children will have to switch to the ________ comprehensive school, which I've heard is awful.

---

switch to – überwechseln auf/in ***comprehensive (school)*** – Gesamtschule

Natur

nature? **countryside?**

natural surroundings? **natural environment?**

Man versus nature

*I love being out in the open – the **countryside**, the mountains, the sea, I can't live without them. But when I see what our "civilized" societies are doing to our **natural environment**, it makes me quite ill. Not even intelligent people seem to understand the most basic **laws of nature**. Don't they realize we weren't put on this earth to conquer **nature** but to live in harmony with her? If people go on destroying the **balance of nature** the way they have been doing, there won't be any **natural surroundings** left for us to enjoy.*

nature

(kein Artikel!) abstrakt/poetisch; die Schöpfung/Naturgewalt
the forces/laws/wonders/balance of nature
mother nature, man and nature, a freak of nature

natural surroundings

natürliche Umgebung, konkret gesehen
Building a motorway link to the airport along here is going to spoil the natural surroundings completely.

natural environment

Umwelt, abstrakt und oft global gesehen
It's our children who will suffer for the crimes we're committing against our natural environment.

the countryside (and the sea/mountains)

Natur, Landschaft als Erlebnis; wird im Englischen präzisiert
He loves being in the countryside / in the mountains. / He loves the mountains and the sea. usw. – Er liebt die Natur.

nature, natural surroundings, natural environment *oder* ***countryside?***

1. *Why don't you go to Tuscany? The ______________ there is beautiful.*
2. *A lot more ought to be done to preserve our ______________.*
3. *These bizarrely shaped rocks are a freak of ______________.*
4. *The island is perfect for nature lovers and sunseekers, offering unspoilt ______________ and plenty of sun.*

---

preserve – erhalten ***sunseeker*** – Sonnenanbeter

Paar

pair? **couple?**

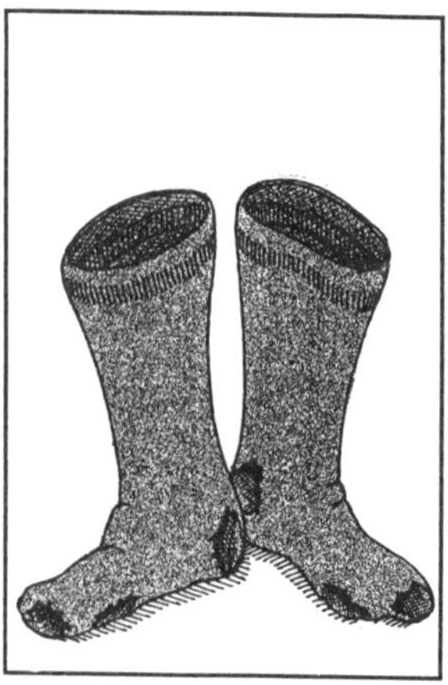

What a pair!

Helmut: *Just look at this, Sally – I bought* ***a new pair of socks*** *last week and they're already full of holes.*

Sally: *Well, a couple of days ago I got myself this expensive* ***pair of boots****, and one of the heels has just come off.*
Helmut: *We do make* ***a fine pair****, don't we? Perhaps we should go to the fancy-dress ball tonight as* ***a penniless couple*** *– the others might feel sorry for us and give us a couple of quid towards some new footwear!*

---

fancy-dress ball – Maskenball ***penniless*** – völlig verarmt ***quid*** – (umgs.) Pfund

a pair (of)

ein Paar (Socken, Schuhe usw.)
Those look like a very sensible pair of shoes. Not quite as fashionable as the other pair, of course.
two pairs of socks – zwei Paar Socken

a couple

meist Mann + Frau, ein (Ehe-)Paar/Liebespaar/Pärchen
the perfect couple – das ideale Paar
Anna and Thomas make such a nice couple.

a pair

(besonders ironisch) ein komisches/lustiges Paar
What a strange pair those two are.

Übrigens:
a couple (of) – (umgs.) ein paar, einige
There were only a couple of people at the pub yesterday lunchtime.
Can you lend me a couple of stamps?

pair *oder* **couple?**

1. *Look at those two elderly people on the bench holding hands – don't they make a sweet _______________?*
2. *I seem to spend an awful lot of time with my head in the snow. Perhaps I ought to buy a _______________ of those compact skis for beginners.*

passen (zu)

fit? **suit?** **go with?** **match?**

Fitting remarks?

Sally: *This dress* ***fits*** *me perfectly – it's just the right size.*
Helmut: *It is a perfect fit, but really it doesn't* ***suit*** *you at all.*
Sally: *You mean I don't look nice in it?*
Helmut: *Well, it shows too much of your legs, and anyway that shocking pink just doesn't* ***go with*** *your red hair.*
Sally: *Really? But it would* ***match*** *my new pink hat …*

---

fitting remark – passende Bemerkung ***shocking pink*** – Pink ***pink*** – rosa

Etwas taktvoller hätte Helmut ruhig sein können, dafür passen seine Bemerkungen – was das Englische angeht – ganz genau, denn bei der Mode gilt allgemein Folgendes:

fit

(jdm.) in der Größe passen; gut sitzen
This hat doesn't fit me any more.

suit s.o.

zu jdm. / jds. Typ passen, jdm. (gut) stehen
I don't think shorts suit you, Grandad.

go with

(gut) passen zu, harmonisieren mit
That green sweater goes well with the colour of your hair, but it doesn't really go with your blue trousers.

match

in Farbe/Form/Stil genau passen (zu), übereinstimmen (mit), abgestimmt sein (auf)
I'm looking for a handbag to match these sandals.
The shirt and jacket match perfectly.

fit, suit, go with *oder* ***match?*** *Setzen Sie die passende Form ein.*

Your new bikini really ______________ you; it ______________ your hair and ______________ your new beach towel perfectly. What a pity it doesn't ______________ you around the hips.

Pause

break? **interval?**

A note of discontent

First cello: *I'm dying for a drink.*
Double bass: *Yes, I could really do with a* ***break*** *too. I wish Mahler hadn't written such endlessly long symphonies.*
First cello: *Don't you hate these concerts where you have just an overture before the* ***interval****, and then you have to play for nearly two hours without a* ***break****. I don't know how I'm going to last.*
Double bass: *Well, if you're so desperate, perhaps you'd better have a drop of this. I got the barman to fill my hip flask up with brandy during the* ***interval****.*
First cello: *Oh, well done! Do you mind if I just hide behind your instrument for a second …*

---

discontent – Unzufriedenheit ***I could do with …*** – ich könnte … gebrauchen ***last*** – es aushalten ***if you're so desperate*** – wenn es so dringend ist ***hip flask*** – Flachmann

break

Pause, durch die man eine Arbeit / eine Tätigkeit / den Unterricht usw. vorübergehend unterbricht, meist um auszuruhen; auch Schulpause, Mittagspause
tea break, lunch break, morning break
I've been revising for three hours – I think I'll have a break and make myself some tea.

Denken Sie an *break* – Unterbrechung.

interval

vorher festgelegte Pause beim Konzert, im Theater usw.
I don't know whether I could sit through Tannhäuser. How many intervals are there?

Übrigens:
am. und im Kino heißt es ***intermission***
im Sport sagt man ***half time***;
at half time – während der Pause

pause

Zögern, kurzes Innehalten beim Reden, Vortragen usw.
After a short pause to blow his nose, he carried on with his deadly boring speech.

break oder **interval?**

1. *Unfortunately we're sitting in different rows, but I'll meet you in the foyer in the* ________________.

2. *I wish we had longer tea* ________________ (pl.). *It would give us a chance to have a little nap.*

3. *Pupils are not allowed to leave the school premises during any of the* ________________ (pl.).

---

nap – Nickerchen ***premises*** – Gelände

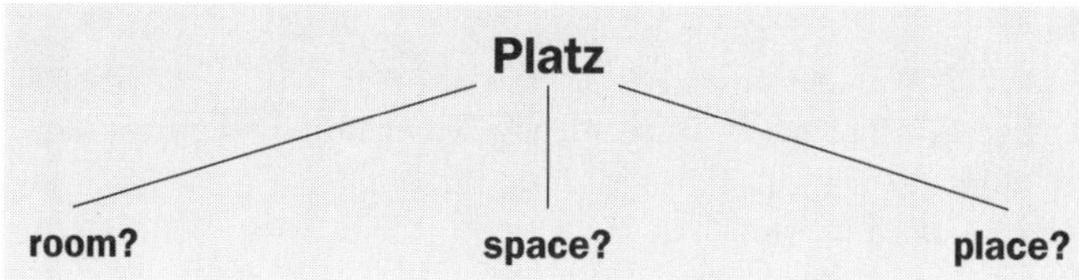

Close encounters

Helmut: *Look, there's* ***a parking space*** *over there, Sally.*
Sally: *I don't think there's enough* ***room*** *for Dad's car.*
Helmut: *There's* ***another space*** *on the other side of the square – we should fit in there.*
Sally: *Let's try that one then, but we'd better hurry otherwise there won't be any seats left at the theatre. Oh dear, I need my glasses for this. Where are they? I hope I didn't leave them lying on your seat, Helmut.*
Helmut: *Haven't I told you a hundred times to keep them* ***in one place****, like your handbag?*
Sally: *But there's no* ***room*** *in this handbag – it's much too small.*
Helmut: *What was that?!*
Sally: *Oh dear, I think I've bumped into the car behind us. Honestly, there really is no* ***room to move*** *in London.*
Helmut: *And it's particularly difficult to judge the* ***limited space available*** *when you're shortsighted and keep forgetting your glasses …*

Diese letzte Bemerkung war vielleicht etwas fehl am Platze, aber die Situation – so unglücklich sie auch sein mag – zeigt uns ganz deutlich den Unterschied zwischen den verschiedenen „Plätzen". Und damit Sie in dieser Sache alle anderen vom Platz fegen können, müssen Sie sich jetzt auf die Erläuterungen voll konzentrieren.

room

verfügbarer Raum/Platz um jd./etwas herum; Bewegungsraum, Freiraum
make room – Platz machen
Well, there's plenty of room in this bed.

space

(ohne *a/an*) hier denkt man an die Abmessungen/Konturen eines Platzes
Is there enough space for this bag between the suitcases?

Wird näher bestimmt:
no space, enough space, hardly any space, take up a lot of space usw.
■ Im Zweifelsfall nehmen Sie ***room***, denn das stimmt fast immer.

a space

ein Platz, eine Lücke, in den/die etwas ziemlich genau hineinpasst
Oh, you've left a space for the baby.

a place

1. eine ganz bestimmte Stelle, wo etwas hingehört
   I've told you before – your place is at the foot of the bed.

2. ein Ort, eine Stelle, ein Plätzchen
   This is a nice place – shall we camp here for a few nights?

Und da wir noch ein bisschen Platz haben:

- ***seat*** – (Sitz-)Platz
  I'd like a window seat, if possible.
- ***square*** – öffentlicher Platz (z. B. *Times Square*)
- ***football pitch*** – Fußballplatz

room, space *oder* ***place?***

"Where on earth can I put this new exercise bike?"
"Well, there's a ________________ there between the desk and your hi-fi equipment. And if you were to put all your records back into their proper ________________ instead of leaving them all over the floor, you'd have plenty of ________________ to do your morning exercises as well."

Reise

trip? **journey?** **voyage?**

There's always a first time

Elderly passenger: *Excuse me, how do I fasten this seatbelt? I've never flown before.*
Businessman: *Really? This must be at least my 200th flight.*
Elderly passenger: *So you're a real globetrotter, then.*
Businessman: *Yes, but it's mostly **business trips**.*
Elderly passenger: *I'm used to travelling by train and boat, but the **voyage** to Australia to see my son and his family would have taken me weeks. It's not like going on a **quick boat trip** across the Channel.*
Businessman: *Well, at least if you had made such a **long journey** by boat, you wouldn't have to worry about jet lag. It can take you days to adjust.*
Elderly passenger: *Talking about adjusting, do you think you could loosen this seatbelt a bit? I can hardly breathe. I wouldn't like this to be my first and last **trip** to Australia.*

trip

Urlaubs- oder Geschäftsreise, auch kürzere
He's away on a business trip.
We occasionally take weekend trips over to Wales.

journey

betont die Fahrt selbst, egal, mit welchem Transportmittel; oft relativ lang oder anstrengend
The journey across the Sahara was rough but fascinating.
How was the journey down from Liverpool?

voyage

lange Reise mit dem Schiff (oder Raumschiff), oft mit Pionier- bzw. Abenteuercharakter (daher relativ seltener Gebrauch)
When I retire I'm going to make a long sea voyage through the Indian Ocean and the Pacific.

Denken Sie an die Raumfähre „*Voyager*".

Aber:
- eine längere Schiffsreise heißt meistens ***cruise*** (= Kreuzfahrt)

Übrigens:

tour – Rundreise
a tour of South Africa – eine Südafrika-Rundreise
Have a good trip! – Gute Reise!

trip, journey *oder* ***voyage?***

1. *When I first met them they were on a honeymoon ______________ to Venice.*
2. *I suggest that after two hours' travelling in this shaky landrover we break our ______________ to stretch our legs and have something to drink.*
3. *We had so many dangerous and exciting experiences on our South American ______________ that it was more like a 17th-century ______________ of discovery.*

Rezept

recipe? **prescription?**

To your health!

Sally: *There's certainly something wrong with this liver of mine, Helmut. I'll really have to get hold of a new* ***recipe****.*
Helmut: *I'll see what I can do.*
(An hour later ...)
Sally: *Where on earth have you been all this time, Helmut? You've missed your dessert, you know.*
Helmut: *I've been to the chemist's to get some medicine for that liver complaint of yours. It was quite expensive – here's the receipt.*
Sally: *My liver complaint?! I wasn't complaining about my liver but the liver we were eating! Anyway, how did you manage to get that medicine over the counter – I mean, without a* ***prescription****?*
Helmut: *A* ***prescription*** *... You mean a recipe?* ☹
Sally: *Well, what I did want was* ***a recipe to cook a new liver dish*** *and not* ***a prescription from the doctor****. My liver's perfectly all right, thank you, particularly as I hardly drink any alcohol, unlike some people I know ...*

---

dessert – Nachtisch ***unlike*** – im Gegensatz zu

Armer Helmut, er hat es wieder gut gemeint, aber leider hat er die Kalbsleber mit Sallys Leber verwechselt, weil er auf eine beliebte Wortverwechslung hereingefallen ist. Unser Rezept dagegen finden Sie im Folgenden.

recipe

Kochrezept; auch Rezept im übertragenen Sinn
Have you got a good recipe for goulash?
Here's yet another book claiming to have the recipe for a successful marriage.

prescription

ärztliches Rezept
Don't forget to fetch Grandma's prescription from the doctor's.

receipt

Kassenbon, Quittung
The receipt's in the bag.

recipe *oder* ***prescription?***

1. *I've forgotten how many teaspoons of curry powder to put into the sauce. I'll have to ask Gill for the ________________ again.*
2. *You hear so many complaints about the very high ________________ charges in Britain, but a lot of people – such as old-age pensioners – don't have to pay anything.*
3. *The young stockbroker next door seems to be a real whizz-kid – he's only 21 and he's made a fortune already. I wonder what his ________________ for success is.*

---

stockbroker – Börsenmakler ***whizz-kid*** – „Senkrechtstarter"

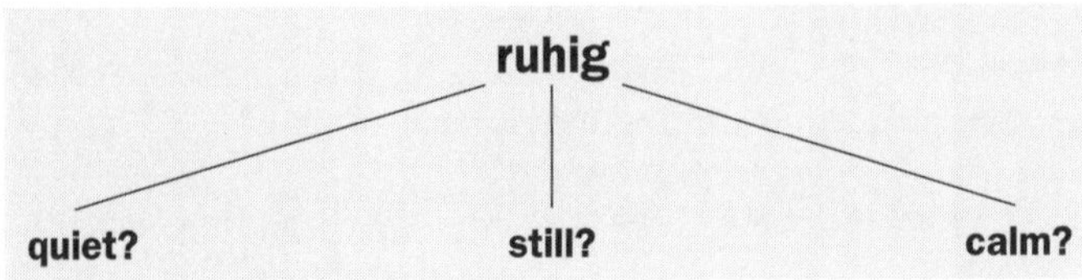

Just sit back and relax

Sally: *You're very* ***quiet*** *this evening, Helmut. You haven't said a word for at least ten minutes.*
Helmut: *Ssh! I'm trying out a new learning method. You have to get into a comfortable position and* ***sit*** *absolutely* ***still****. After a while, when you* ***feel*** *completely* ***calm*** *and relaxed, you switch on the cassette recorder and listen to your next English lesson. And afterwards you find you remember everything.*
Sally: *It sounds like a super learning method. But what happens if you fall asleep before you switch the recorder on? ... Helmut? I said what happens ... Oh well, I suppose it'll be a very* ***quiet*** *evening now.*

quiet

1. leise, still, keinen Lärm erzeugend; schweigsam
   be quiet, keep quiet
   You're very quiet this morning – what's up?
2. ungestört, beschaulich
   I'm looking forward to a quiet weekend on my own.

still

bewegungslos, ruhig (Gegenteil: unruhig); meist in Fügungen wie: *sit still, stand still* usw.
Keep still while I'm cutting your hair!

calm

gelassen, nicht aufgeregt
stay/keep calm – die Ruhe bewahren, ruhig bleiben
cool, calm and collected – ganz ruhig und gelassen
The pilot managed to stay perfectly calm throughout the hijacking.

quiet, still *oder* ***calm?***

Be ________________, you lot! And sit ________________, will you, until this programme's finished. How am I supposed to watch Richard Chamberlain with you children jumping up and down on the settee making animal noises? I don't know how anyone is expected to stay ________________ and not lose their temper with a noisy bunch of kids like you.

---

settee – Sofa

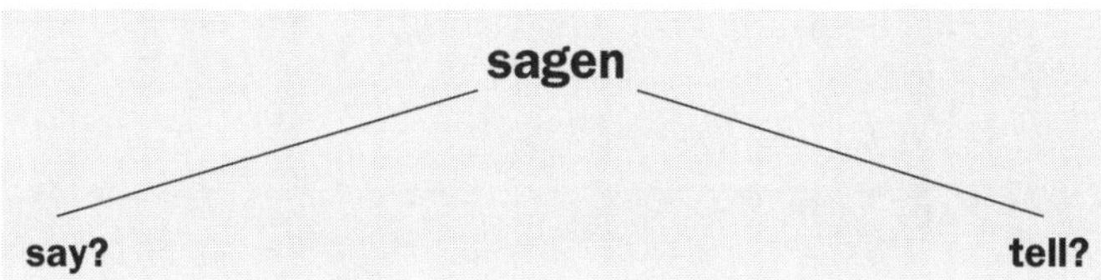

Between you and me …

Ethel: *Do you know **what** Janice **said**?*
Hilda: *No, **what** did she **say** this time?*
Ethel: *Well, she **said that** Josie and Bill had a terrible row at the club last night and that Josie wants a divorce.*
Hilda: *Ethel, I've **told you** before not to listen to all that stupid gossip. After all, couples often argue. It doesn't mean a thing.*
Ethel: *That's **what** you **say**. But Janice **told me**, in confidence of course, that she saw Josie talking to Harry Evans, and everyone knows they used to be keen on each other.*
Hilda: *For heaven's sake, Ethel, I don't know how many times I've **told you** not to repeat **what** Janice **says**. You know she hardly ever **tells the truth**.*
Ethel: *Well, let's wait and see. And don't be surprised when it's my turn to **say** "I **told you** so"!*

---

row – [raʊ] Streit ***divorce*** – Scheidung ***in confidence*** – im Vertrauen ***be keen on*** – „stehen auf"

say

1. wird benutzt, wenn keine Ergänzung mehr folgt; hier bildet es sozusagen das Schlusslicht eines Satzes
   That's exactly what I said.
2. ***say + that***
   She said that she was going home.
   (Hier könnte man auch das *that* weglassen.)

   Eine Person als nachfolgende Ergänzung ist nur möglich, wenn sie mit ***to*** angehängt wird:
   She said to him that she was going home.
   Aber hier bevorzugt man ohnehin ***tell***, da es weniger schwerfällig klingt:
   She told him (that) she was going home.

tell

1. verlangt immer eine unmittelbare Ergänzung (Objekt), entweder eine Person oder etwas Abstraktes (*the truth* usw.)
   I told him that I wasn't coming to the wedding.
   She never tells the truth.
2. wird verwendet bei einer Aufforderung, etwas zu tun oder zu unterlassen
   I told her not to smoke in bed.

Im Passiv: *She was told not to smoke in bed.*

***say** oder **tell?** Setzen Sie die passende Form ein.*

1. *Chris ____________ that she often suffers from jet lag when she comes back from the States, but not the other way round.*

2. *She ____________ him to be quiet.*

3. *He ____________ me that he'd always been afraid of flying and ____________ that he avoided travelling by plane whenever he could.*

Salat

lettuce? **salad?**

The right mix

Customer: *Waiter, I've just ordered this **salad**. I thought this was said to be a first-class vegetarian restaurant.*
Waiter: *Yes, sir – radishes, tomatoes, cucumber, **lettuce** and chives, all garden-fresh.*
Customer: *So that's how you explain the presence of these meaty slugs, is it?*
Waiter: *But there's no extra charge, sir.*

---

chives – Schnittlauch ***slug*** – (Nackt-)Schnecke

Und hier noch einmal der ganze Salat:

lettuce

(Kopf-)Salat
We've grown some nice lettuces in the garden.
iceberg lettuce – Eissalat

salad

angemachter Salat
tomato/mixed/chicken salad
side salad – Salat als Beilage

lettuce *oder* ***salad?***

"Stop picking around in your ________________ and eat it up. It's full of vitamins."
"But I hate onions, and I told you just to give me the cucumber and ________________ without any onion."

Schatten

shadow? — **shade?**

shadow

der deutlich umrissene Schatten, den ein Mensch/Gegenstand usw. wirft
I saw a man's shadow against the wall.

shade

der Schatten als Schutz vor der Sonne (nur im Singular)
It's 30 degrees in the shade.

Denken Sie beim längeren ***shadow*** an den langen Schatten, den man wirft; beim kürzeren ***shade*** denken Sie an Schutz.

shadow *oder* ***shade?***

1. *You can tell it's autumn – the days are getting shorter and the ______________ (pl.) longer.*

2. *If you haven't put any suntan lotion on I think you'd better go and sit in the ______________, otherwise you're going to get sunburnt.*

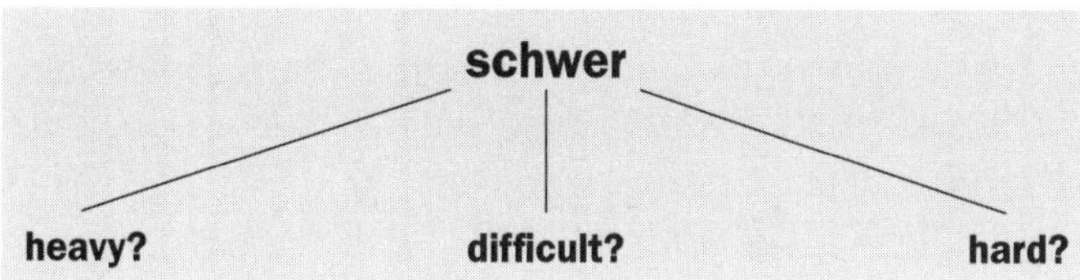

It's a hard life

Brenda: *Hello, Alec. Have you been waiting long?*
Alec: *No, I've just arrived. How are you?*
Brenda: *I'm worn out – I've had such a* ***hard*** *day. I seem to get all the really* ***heavy*** *projects at work. Do you think you could hold this for me while I look for my key?*
Alec: *Gosh, this bag's really* ***heavy****. What on earth have you got in it – a ton of bricks?*
Brenda: *No, just three dictionaries. The translation I'm doing is so* ***difficult*** *and I made quite a few bad mistakes in the first chapter, so I was in trouble with my boss. I've decided to do some of it at home to be on the safe side.*
Alec: *Oh, Brenda. Life's* ***hard*** *enough without ruining your evenings with work as well.*

Ja, das Leben ist schon schwer. Und wenn es Ihnen auch schwer fällt, um die Erklärungen kommen wir leider nicht herum.

heavy

1. von großem Gewicht
   She had to drag the suitcase along the ground because it was so heavy.
2. schwer im übertragenen Sinn; auch schwer verdaulich
   a heavy meal/wine/storm
   heavy reading, heavy losses
   He had a heavy cold, so he stayed off work for a few days.

difficult

schwierig, kompliziert (etwas gehobener als *hard*)
I always find it so difficult to fill in my tax forms.

hard

1. schwierig, schwer zu vollziehen
   Is it really so hard for you to decide?
2. anstrengend
   The place was in such a mess, it was a hard job getting it tidied up.

Übrigens:
In der Bedeutung „schwierig" sind ***difficult*** und ***hard*** oft austauschbar.

heavy, difficult *oder* ***hard?***

Times are getting ________________ er for the police as the number of bad accidents on the motorways increases daily. Only this morning a ________________ lorry crashed into a car parked on the hard shoulder. It was very ________________ for the police to free the trapped passengers, several of whom had to receive emergency treatment in a nearby hospital.

---

hard shoulder – Standspur

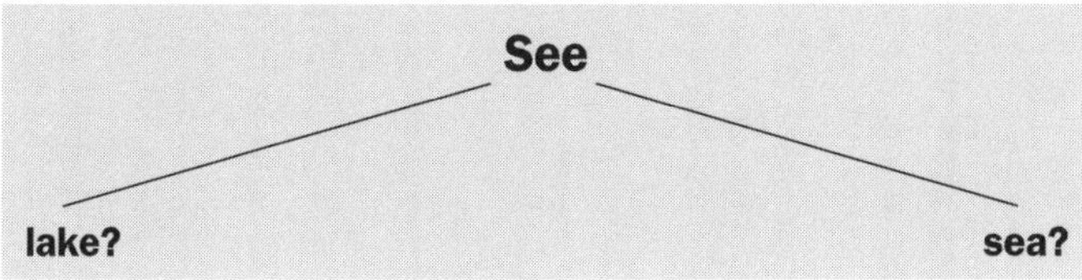

der See

die See

Denken Sie beim See *(lake)* an die Regenlache, die ja relativ klein ist, oder an den Loch Ness.

lake *oder* ***sea?***

1. *Look, there's Dad on the other side of the ______________.*

2. *The ______________ air around here isn't what it used to be.*

3. *It only took us a few hours to drive around ______________ Garda.*

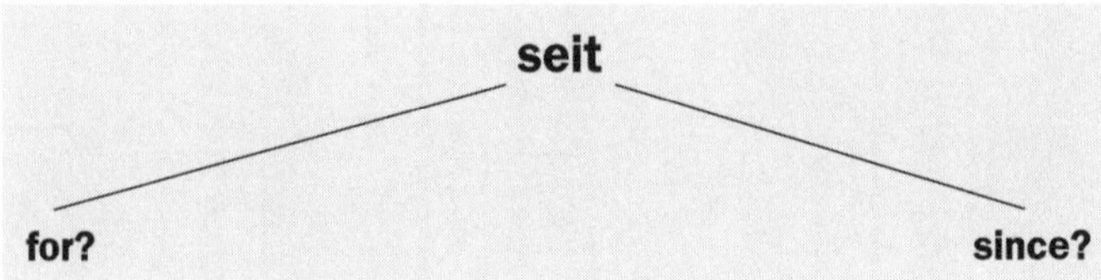

Thirsty work!

Peter: *It's only eight o'clock and Helmut's been drinking* ***for the last two hours – ever since the pub opened at six****.*
Sally: *Yes, I know. He's drunk at least four pints* ***since I arrived****. He claims he has to spend a lot of time in the pub to get plenty of English practice.*
Peter: ***For years*** *he's been complaining that English beer is flat, tasteless and lukewarm, but* ***ever since he discovered Guinness*** *he's been drinking it almost non-stop!*

---

flat – schal ***lukewarm*** – lauwarm

for

Zeit**dauer**
Angabe der Zeitdauer, meist durch eine Konstruktion mit ***a/an*** bzw. mit Zeitangabe im Plural (*-s*):

for a week
for an hour
for a long time
for five days
for hundreds of years
for ages

since

Zeit**punkt**
genaue Angabe der Uhrzeit, des Tages usw. oder einer Handlung bzw. eines Ereignisses:

since 9 o'clock
since last Monday
since January
since 1963
since he was born
since I last saw you

for oder **since?**

Helmut has been learning English ____________ a long time.
Helmut has been learning English ____________ 1981.
Helmut has been learning English ____________ years.
Helmut has been learning English ____________ he was 14.
Helmut has drunk five pints ____________ the pub opened.

so

so? **such?** **like this/that?**

The party's over

Helmut: *Oh Sally, I'm* ***so tired*** *and there's still such a lot to clear up.*
Sally: *Well, I must say I've never seen the kitchen in* ***such an awful mess****, but we should have it all done by the morning. Er, Helmut, you don't put the glasses in the dishwasher* ***like that****; you have to put them in upside down –* ***like this****, see?*

Helmut: *Sorry. I'm* ***so stupid*** *sometimes. I think you'd better do the rest before I break something. Goodnight, Sally!*
Sally: *He may be a good cook, but I've never known a man* ***like that*** *for getting out of housework!*

---

get out of – sich drücken vor

So geht's natürlich nicht. Mit **solchen** Drückebergern haben wir doch nichts gemein, oder? Da wir **so** fleißig sind, machen wir uns denn auch sofort an die Details heran:

so + Adjektiv/Adverb

The play was so good, and all the children acted so well.

such (+ a/an) (+ Adjektiv) + Substantiv – solch

He's such a nice person.
They're such noisy animals.

Das Adjektiv kann bei Substantiven mit emotionalem Gehalt entfallen:
such a mess, such a fuss, such idiots

like this, like that

vergleichend:

1. solch/so (ein/eine usw.), diese Art von
   I wish we had a car like that.
2. so, auf diese Weise
   You don't eat it like that, you eat it like this.

so, such oder ***like this?***

She's ____________ self-confident and thinks she knows ____________ a lot. She really makes me feel ____________ an idiot all the time. If it goes on ____________ for much longer, I'm going to leave.

sportlich

sporty? **sporting / sports …?** **athletic?**

From the small ads

*Eligible bachelor (26), intelligent, multilingual, good-looking, **athletic**, seeks similarly attractive, **sporty** young lady to play tennis, go skiing and share other **sporting activities** with.*
Replies with photo to Helmut, Box no. XYZ 007.

---

small ads – Kleinanzeigen ***eligible bachelor*** – begehrter Junggeselle ***box number*** – Chiffre(nummer)

Und nun für Sie ein bisschen Denksport:

sporty

1. (Person; etwas umgs.) sportlich;
   „sportlich sein" heißt jedoch meistens:
   be keen on sport(s) / do a lot of sport(s)
2. (Kleidung) salopp-sportlich, lässig; oft auch *casual*
   I know you like to wear sporty clothes, but I don't think we should dress too casually for Dad's 60th birthday.

sporting

1. (Dinge, Abstraktes; auch ***sports …***) sportlich, Sport …
   The new sports centre offers a wide range of sporting activities for young and old.
2. (auch ***sportsmanlike***) im übertragenen Sinn sportlich, fair
   It's very sporting of you not to charge me for the crate of whisky I dropped.

athletic

1. (Körperbau) athletisch
   I love tall, athletic men.
2. (bes. Mann) sportlich
   My boys are all very athletic.

Übrigens:

- ***sports gear/kit*** – Sportsachen
- ***sportswear*** – Sportbekleidung
- ***sports/sporting page*** – Sportteil (in der Zeitung)

sportive bedeutet etwa „verspielt“, ist aber kein sehr geläufiges Wort

sporty, sporting, sports *oder* ***athletic?***

My husband is quite an ________________ person, and he's always away at some ________________ event or other. I've never been a ________________ type myself. I get plenty of exercise, though, with all the housework I do – especially when it comes to washing and ironing the piles of filthy sports gear Bruce regularly brings home from his rugby matches. If he was a bit more ________________, he would do it himself.

stören

bother? **disturb?** **spoil?**

Don't be such a spoilsport

Mr Travers: *I'm sorry to* ***bother you****, but do you think you could park your coach a bit further down the road, out of sight? It's* ***spoiling the view*** *of the valley from here.*

Mr Bradley: *Oh, sorry about that. I didn't think it would* ***bother anyone****.*
Mr Travers: *It's not only that. The sound of the engine when you drive off at the crack of dawn every morning* ***disturbs my sleep****.*
Mr Bradley: *I'm glad you mentioned it, because I just told two of my mates they could park here as well.*
Mr Travers: *Well, I'm sorry to spoil your fun, but I did buy my house here for some peace and quiet and unspoilt countryside, after all.*

---

spoilsport – Spielverderber ***coach*** – Reisebus ***at the crack of dawn*** – in aller Herrgottsfrühe ***mate*** – Kumpel

bother

1. (jd.) belästigen; kommt oft in Höflichkeitsfloskeln vor
   I hate to bother you, but could you lend me some milk?
2. (jd.) stören, irritieren, (jdm.) etwas ausmachen
   Most people complain about the noisy traffic around here, but it doesn't really bother me.

disturb

1. (die Ruhe, den Schlaf, die Konzentration usw.) stören
   Can't you put those noisy birds somewhere else? They're disturbing my concentration.
2. (jd. bei der Arbeit, beim Schlafen usw.) stören
   Try to go up the stairs quietly so as not to disturb the baby.
   Am I disturbing you? – Störe ich (gerade)?

spoil

(die Harmonie, etwas Harmonisches) (zer)stören, beeinträchtigen, verderben
That new office block over there completely spoils the mediaeval character of the town centre.

bother, disturb *oder* ***spoil?*** *Setzen Sie die passende Form ein.*

1. *It doesn't really ______________ me that you come home after midnight every night, but I wish you wouldn't ______________ everybody by slamming the car door.*

2. *I hate to have to ______________ you with yet another problem, but could you possibly look after my three cats this weekend?*

3. *I got into trouble for hanging my washing out last Sunday. The people next door complained bitterly that it was ______________ their view of the back gardens.*

Straße

road? **street?**

Streetwise

Mrs T.: *I wouldn't let my children play out* ***in the streets*** *on their own – there's just too much traffic* ***on the roads****.*
Mrs B.: *And all those* ***street people*** *with nowhere to live.*
Mrs T.: *Not to mention the* ***street gangs*** *– I'm so worried about getting mugged that I always avoid the* ***side-streets*** *at night. Even if I'm in the car I try and stick to the* ***main roads****.*
Mrs B.: *And then you're not safe from all those maniac drivers who think they own the* ***roads****.*
Mrs T.: *Yes. And isn't it funny how all the* ***roadhogs*** *seem to be men too?*

---

be streetwise – sich im harten Alltag durchschlagen können ***get mugged*** – auf der Straße überfallen und beraubt werden ***roadhog*** – Straßenrowdy

road

1. Verbindung zwischen einem Punkt A und B (außerhalb oder innerhalb einer Ortschaft); Straße nach/zum/zur …
   She lived in a terraced house off the main Liverpool to Manchester road.
   Does this road go to the station?
2. in Verbindung mit dem Fahren, dem Verkehr, der Straßenverkehrsordnung, den Straßenverhältnissen usw.; die Fahrbahn steht im Vordergrund
   road safety, road construction, roadworks, a road test

street

nur innerhalb einer geschlossenen Ortschaft, vor allem aber in Verbindung mit dem Leben und dem menschlichen Treiben auf der Straße
a street market, a street cleaner
street life, street fighting, street gangs
the man in the street
On Saturdays the streets are swarming with people doing their weekend shopping.

street – Straße mit Bürgersteig

---

terraced house – Reihenhaus ***be swarming with*** – wimmeln von

road *oder* ***street?***

1. *In winter the ____________ conditions in this part of Scotland can be quite bad.*

2. *Customs officers have seized drugs with an estimated __________ value of one million pounds.*

3. *It's a long way by ____________. Why don't you fly?*

4. *They should provide some sort of community centre for all these unemployed youngsters who just hang around ____________ corners all day.*

---

seize – beschlagnahmen ***community centre*** – Gemeindezentrum

streng

strict? **severe?**

Doctor's orders

Helmut: *The doctor had rather a* ***severe expression*** *on his face when he left.*
Sally: *Yes, I know. He's very cross with Dad because he refuses to follow the* ***strict diet*** *he prescribed. It's no wonder Dad is in such terrible pain. Perhaps we ought to be a bit* ***stricter*** *when he asks for his favourite cream cakes and brandy!*

Leider sind hier die englischen Begriffe gar nicht so streng auseinander zu halten. Mithilfe einiger typischer Zusammensetzungen wollen wir Ihnen aber über den Berg helfen.

strict

Regeln konsequent befolgend; strenge Disziplin verlangend
strict instructions/rules/discipline
a strict Catholic/vegetarian
strict parents, a strict teacher
a strict upbringing/diet

Und:
strictly confidential/prohibited – streng vertraulich/verboten

severe

hart, unerbittlich
a severe look/expression/winter
a severe sentence/punishment/judge
severe criticism/implications

⚠ Verwechseln Sie das deutsche Wort „streng“ nicht mit dem englischen *strong*!

a strong man

a strict teacher

✎ ***strict*** *oder* ***severe?***

In Britain the image of the ________________ schoolmaster with a ________________ expression on his face has disappeared. Punishments for pupils' bad behaviour have become less ________________ too, and the cane has been banned. However, many people believe that the lack of ________________ discipline in schools is one of the major causes of juvenile delinquency.

---

cane – Rohrstock ***juvenile deliquency*** – Jugendkriminalität

Technik

technology? **technical matters?**

engineering? **technique?**

High-tech in the home

Peter: *If you ask me, all this **modern technology** in the home just makes life more complicated. I can't even get the dishwasher open, never mind get it to work.*
Mrs Wilson: *Look, there's a very **simple technique**: you turn the knob to the right, press it in, let it go again to release the lock, and the door opens – it's child's play.*
Peter: *I never was very good at **technical things**.*
Mrs Wilson: *Well, I remember not so long ago you were planning a career in **electrical engineering**. What made you change your mind?*
Peter: *All the mod cons and contraptions in this house!*
Mrs Wilson: *I've always maintained that women can cope better when it comes to **technical matters**.*

it's child's play – es ist kinderleicht ***mod cons*** – moderne Gerätschaften (Abkürzung für ***modern conveniences***) ***contraptions*** – „Apparatur“ ***maintain*** – behaupten

Tja, die Übersetzung von „Technik“ scheint fast so kompliziert zu sein wie die moderne Technik selbst. Also aufgepasst!

technology

(ohne Artikel) Technologie; die Technik im weitesten Sinn; eher der theoretische/abstrakte Begriff
There have been some amazing developments in technology in recent decades.

engineering

(ohne Artikel)

1. Technik in der Praxis
   The Aswan Dam is still considered to be one of the great achievements of engineering in the 20th century.
2. zur Bezeichnung von Teilbereichen aus der Technik
   genetic engineering – Gentechnik
   electrical engineering – Elektrotechnik
   civil engineering – Hoch- und Tiefbau

technique

„Technik", Vorgehensweise, Methode, mit der etwas ausgeführt wird; bezieht sich häufig auch auf „nicht technische" Dinge
There's a certain technique to working Dad's video recorder.
You must pay more attention to your technique when you practise the piano.

technical things/matters

Technik, wobei die technischen Geräte und ihre Handhabung im Vordergrund stehen
I haven't got a clue about technical matters.

technology, engineering, technique *oder* ***technical matters?***

Am I really hopeless when it comes to ______________, or is there some special ______________ to getting this radio to work? If my husband would only take advantage of what modern ______________ has to offer these days, I wouldn't have to waste my time messing around with this pre-war radio and a black-and-white TV set with only two channels. If I was the breadwinner in this house, we'd have all the latest ______________ – a decent hi-fi system, a remote-control television with teletext, and an automatic washing machine and tumble-drier for Brian. Still, I suppose it's my own fault for getting married instead of finishing my electrical ______________ degree.

---

breadwinner – Geldverdiener ***remote-control …*** – … mit Fernbedienung ***degree*** – Studium ***tumble-drier*** – Wäschetrockner

Termin

appointment? **date?** **deadline?**

Getting organized

Mr Wilson: *Have you seen my diary anywhere? I* ***made an appointment*** *to see the dentist and I have a feeling I should have gone yesterday.*
Sally: *Oh, Dad, you're always losing your diary and forgetting* ***appointments****. If I* ***fix a date*** *to see someone, I make sure I remember. If you've got so many* ***appointments to keep*** *and* ***deadlines to meet*** *you've got to get yourself organized. Why don't you buy one of those big leather diaries and glue it to your desk?*

appointment

Termin beim Arzt, beim Friseur, zum Vorstellungsgespräch usw.
Jonathan's getting such bad marks at school, I must make an appointment with his headmaster.

date

1. vereinbarter/festgelegter Tag einer Verabredung, Sitzung, Lieferung usw.
   Can we fix a time and date for the next meeting?
2. Rendezvous, Verabredung
   I've finally got a date with Mark – he's asked me out to dinner on Friday!

deadline

Fristablauf; Termin als letzte Möglichkeit, etwas einzureichen / zu erledigen usw.
I'd better get a move on – next week is the deadline for handing in my application.

---

get a move on – „sich sputen" ***application*** – Bewerbung, Antrag

appointment, date *oder* ***deadline?***

1. *The writer was under tremendous pressure from her publisher – the ________________ for handing in the manuscript of her latest novel was only a month away.*
2. *The manager has been taken seriously ill. His secretary is having to cancel all his ________________* (pl.).
3. *I'm afraid the meeting will have to be postponed to a later ________________.*

publisher – Verleger, Verlag ***cancel*** – absagen ***postpone*** – aufschieben

tödlich

fatal? **lethal?** **deadly?**

fatal?	lethal?	deadly?
disease	–	*disease*
–	*poison*	*poison*
–	*weapon*	*weapon*
trap	–	*trap*
accident	*medicine*	–
injury	*dose*	*danger*
wound	*effect*	–
shot/fall/blow usw.	–	–

Dead and gone

We thought he must have died in a ***fatal accident*** *or of some* ***deadly*** *exotic* ***disease****. In fact he was found to have been dealing in the export of* ***lethal weapons*** *to the Middle East. Realizing he was now in mortal danger, he had decided to take his own life by injecting a* ***lethal dose*** *of morphine.*

Verzeihen Sie das „tödliche" Thema, aber das Wort hat es in sich. Wir können Ihnen zwar keine todsicheren Tipps geben, dafür aber einige lebenswichtige Hinweise, die Sie vor fatalen Fehlern bewahren sollen.

fatal

mit tödlichem Ausgang
The foreign minister suffered fatal injuries in the bomb attack.

lethal

potenziell tödlich; klingt sachlicher als *deadly*
If taken in high doses, this medicine can have a lethal effect.

deadly

1. potenziell tödlich; klingt dramatisch/bedrohlich
   That new bread knife you bought looks like a deadly weapon!
2. (im übertragenen Sinn, umgs.) tödlich, unerträglich
   It was such a deadly party, I nearly fell asleep.

   Oft auch vor einem Adjektiv:
   deadly boring – todlangweilig

Übrigens:
mortal klingt literarisch/dramatisch und erscheint in folgenden Kombinationen:
mortal danger/wound/combat

fatal, lethal *oder* ***deadly?***

1. *This cabinet contains various ____________ poisons, so keep it locked at all times.*
2. *Three of the people involved in yesterday's pile-up on the M1 suffered ____________ injuries.*
3. *The guerrilla troops walked straight into the ____________ trap.*

---

pile-up – Massenkarambolage ***M1*** – Autobahn von London in Richtung Norden

tragen

wear? **carry?**

What a carry-on!

If there's one thing I can't stand it's having to ***carry*** *a handbag. Why can't the fashion designers produce practical clothes for women to* ***wear*** *as well? I mean clothes with pockets big enough to* ***carry*** *all your bits and pieces in – such as your sunglasses, which you end up* ***wearing*** *all day and night because you can't fit them into your wretched handbag anyway.*

What a carry-on! – So ein Palaver! ***wretched*** – verflucht

wear

(Kleidung, Schmuck, Brille usw.) anhaben, aufhaben, umhaben
I hope Grandma doesn't turn up at my 21st birthday party wearing her new jeans.

carry

tragen (in der Hand, auf dem Rücken, in der Tasche/Handtasche usw.); dabeihaben
The women carry their babies on their backs while they work.
I always carry my allergy ID on me.

ID – Ausweis

wear *oder* ***carry?*** *Setzen Sie die passende Form ein.*

1. *Why is it that visitors to London still expect the average businessman in the City to ____________ a bowler hat and ____________ an umbrella?*

2. *Is that his real hair, or is he ____________ a wig?*

3. *With that heavy bride's dress and all the jewellery you're planning to ____________, I don't know whether I'm going to be able to ____________ you over the threshold.*

---

threshold – Türschwelle

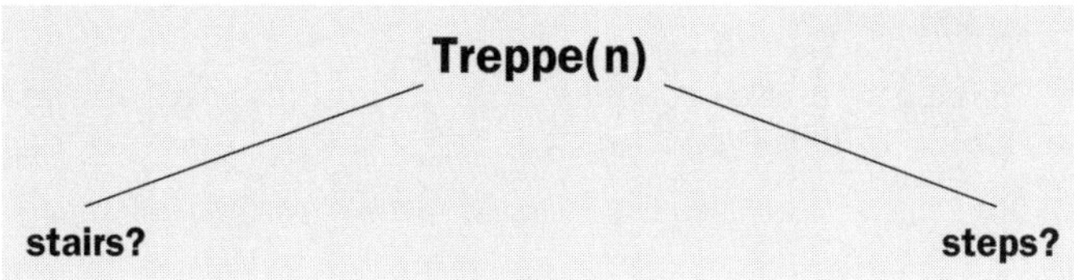

A step in the right direction

*I find it so hard climbing **stairs**, not to mention having to carry heavy shopping up to my flat on the fourth floor. Why can't they put us old folks in proper houses? I could just about manage the **steps** leading up to the front door. Perhaps I should go to Dr Martin's phobia classes after all – she might be able to cure me of my fear of lifts. It's a pity her surgery's on the 12th floor …*

floor – Etage, Stock(werk)   ***surgery*** – Praxis

stairs

Treppe(n) im Haus oder Wohnblock
The carpet on these stairs is so slippery – I'm surprised nobody's fallen down them yet.

steps

Treppe(n) aus Stein, folglich oft draußen
When I came home I found my husband sitting on the front steps. He had locked himself out.

Übrigens:

flight (of stairs) – Treppe, Etage, Stockwerk
Mr Davies lives two flights further up.

stairs** oder **steps?

1. *Do you have to slide down the __________ on your backside? You'll ruin your new pyjamas.*
2. *The __________ leading up to the castle are steep and slippery.*
3. *If he's in a wheelchair, it's no good putting him in a house with two flights of __________.*

Übung

practice? — **(an) exercise?**

A little bit every day

Helmut: *I've got my English test coming up very soon and I feel my grammar's a bit rusty. I'm just out of **practice**.*
Sally: *There's not much wrong with your grammar as far as I can see. But if you want, we can do some **exercises** from your grammar book together. I'm sure half an hour's **practice** a day would be more than enough.*
Helmut: *Do you think I'll be able to brush it up in time for the test?*
Sally: *I'm sure you will. Remember, **practice** makes perfect!*

rusty – eingerostet ***brush up*** – auffrischen

practice

das Üben; regelmäßige Wiederholung zum Zweck des Lernens / der Verbesserung
Learning to ski well is just a matter of practice.

practice makes perfect
(Übung macht den Meister!)

an exercise

eine <u>einzelne</u> Übung (geistige/sportliche/sprachliche usw.); eine Aufgabe
This is a good exercise on future tenses.
Be careful not to strain your back when you're doing your keep-fit exercises.

exercise

(ohne *an*!) = körperliche Bewegung
Too many people sit in an office all day long and don't get any exercise at all.

Und jetzt, wie üblich, eine kleine Übung:

practice *oder* ***exercise?***

1. *The neighbours were driven mad by the girl next door doing her* ________________ (pl.) *on the violin.*

2. *If you want to speak Russian fluently, you'll need a lot of* ________________.

3. *For homework will you please do the* ________________ *on page five.*

verboten

not allowed? **prohibited?** **forbidden?** **...?**

We wish you a pleasant flight

Air hostess: *Do you think you could sit up properly and fasten your seatbelt, please?* ***You're not allowed to*** *be lying down during the landing approach. And there's* ***no smoking*** *in this section of the plane.*
Passenger: *Er, could I just go to the toilet?*

Air hostess: *If you're quick. And remember – **smoking** in the lavatories and aisles **is absolutely forbidden**.*
Passenger: *I also wanted to take a picture of the pilot before we land.*
Air hostess: *Sorry, **no photographs** in the cockpit.*
Passenger: *Well, I think I'll just quietly listen to my little radio over the earphones, if that's all right.*
Air hostess: *I'm afraid radios are **strictly prohibited**, but you can listen to the music provided as part of our in-flight entertainment service.*
Passenger: *Are you absolutely sure? After all, I wouldn't like to do anything on this plane that's **not allowed** …*

---

aisle – Gang ***shot*** – Schuss, Foto ***in-flight entertainment*** – Bordunterhaltung

Folgende Ausführungen sehen zugegebenermaßen ziemlich verboten aus. Aber Überspringen ist streng verboten!

you're not allowed to … … is/are not allowed

Die häufigsten Übersetzungen von „es ist verboten zu …/… ist verboten“:
You're not allowed to wear shorts in this restaurant. / Shorts are not allowed in this restaurant.
(Auf keinen Fall: *It is not allowed to …* ☹!)

no smoking, no spitting, no rollerskating
no skateboards, no photographs, no entry
„… verboten!“

it is prohibited to … … is/are prohibited

„es ist (strengstens) verboten/untersagt zu …/… ist/sind (strengstens) verboten/untersagt“

smoking prohibited
„Rauchen verboten!“
klingt gehoben bzw. offiziell

it is forbidden to …   … is/are forbidden

klingt bedrohlicher bzw. ist schriftsprachlich/gehoben; oft mit moralisch-religiösem Beigeschmack
In this part of the country it's forbidden for women to show their hair in public.

not allowed, prohibited *oder* ***forbidden?***

1. *Smoking ______________. Penalty £50.*
2. *Children are ______________ to play in the courtyard.*
3. *Why should women still have to suffer because Adam was tempted by the ______________ fruit thousands of years ago?*

während

while? **during?**

Did you have a nice trip?

It was a disaster from beginning to end. ***While I was boarding*** *the plane my straw hat flew off and landed in a pool of oil on the tarmac.* ***During the flight*** *one of the air hostesses spilt a whole tray of sticky orange juice all over me. Then* ***while I was going through customs*** *at the other end, my case burst open and everything fell out. But don't imagine that was all:* ***during the two weeks*** *I was there it snowed non-stop. That's definitely the last time I'm going to St Petersburg* ***during the Easter holidays****.*

tarmac – Rollfeld ***tray*** – Tablett ***sticky*** – klebrig

while + Verb

while they were watching TV, while I was asleep

during + Substantiv

das einen meist fest umrissenen Zeitabschnitt beinhaltet
during the lesson/exam/programme/strike

during + Ding

Das deutsche „während“ + Substantiv wird im Englischen oft durch eine Verbalkonstruktion wiedergegeben:
while he was away – während seiner Abwesenheit
while we were having dinner – während des Abendessens
while I was at university – während meines Studiums

Formeller wären hier: *during his absence, during the meal, during my time at university.*

while *oder* ***during?***

1. *Do you children have to jump around and make noises like chimpanzees ____________ I'm trying to teach you the theory of evolution? Can't you do it ____________ the lunch break?*
2. ____________ *the ambulance strike, people had to be taken to hospital in taxis.*

wenn

when? **if?**

If or when …

Helmut: *When* *I pass my final English test, I'm going to take you all out for a slap-up meal.*
Sally: *You're very sure of yourself, Helmut. Don't you mean* ***if*** *you pass?*

Helmut: *Well, Sally, you've always been so good at pointing out my mistakes that I feel quite confident about my English now. Of course I'm not perfect, but I know you'll correct me* ***if*** *I make any more mistakes.*
Sally: *You mean* ***when*** *you make your* ***next*** *mistake …*

---

slap-up meal – tolles Essen ***confident*** – selbstsicher

Wenn das Wörtchen „wenn" nicht wär, wär das Leben halb so schwer …

when

zeitlich; es steht fest, dass etwas geschehen wird
When I buy the computer I'll be broke.
Die Entscheidung ist schon getroffen: nach dem Kauf wird der Käufer pleite sein.

when antwortet auf die Frage „wann?"

if

es ist noch offen, ob etwas passieren wird
If I buy the computer I'll be broke.
Es ist nicht sicher, ob der Computer gekauft wird; nur falls dies geschieht, wird der Käufer pleite sein.

if = falls

when *oder* ***if?***

1. ____________ *you've got any time on Saturday, perhaps you could come round and show me how my computer works.*
2. *Later on,* ____________ *you've finished in the garden, you can start peeling the potatoes.*
3. ____________ *I ever learn to speak English properly, I'm going to emigrate to Australia.*

werden

go? **get?**

It's all getting a bit much

Kevin: *Have you* ***gone*** *completely* ***mad****? Who's supposed to eat all this food? It'll* ***go bad*** *in this muggy weather.*
Rosi: *Did you say something, Kev?*
Kevin: *I think you must be* ***going deaf*** *as well. I said, all this food you bought will* ***go off*** *in the hot weather!*
Rosi: *There's no need to* ***get*** *so* ***cross****. I just* ***got sick and tired*** *of coming home to an empty fridge every evening.*
Kevin: *But I thought you were the one who was worried about* ***getting fat****. And so you should be.*
Rosi: *I'm not so much worried about putting on weight any more as* ***going grey*** *with your non-stop nagging …*

---

muggy – schwül (auch ***close***, ***sticky***)   ***nag*** – herumnörgeln, -mäkeln

Bei „werden" wird es jetzt leider etwas länger werden. Damit es aber nicht zu viel wird, beschränken wir uns auf einige repräsentative Übersetzungen.

go

go deaf	taub werden	*go sour*	sauer werden
go blind	blind werden	*go bad/off*	schlecht werden
go bald	kahl werden	*go pale*	blass werden
go grey	grau werden	*go white*	weiß werden
go mad	verrückt werden	*go red*	rot werden

⚠ Bei *go* liegt die Betonung eher auf dem Endzustand, der sich oft drastisch vom Ausgangszustand unterscheidet.

In manchen Fällen kann man *go* durch das etwas gehobenere *turn* ersetzen: *turn sour/pale/grey/white/cold.*

get

get dark	dunkel werden	*get sick*	krank werden
get cold	kalt werden	*get tired*	müde werden
get warm/hot	warm werden	*get weak*	schwach werden
get wet	nass werden	*get old*	alt werden
get fat	dick werden	*get/fall ill*	krank werden
get rich	reich werden	*get worse*	schlimmer werden
		get better	besser werden

get cross/angry/mad wütend werden
get sick and tired of s.th. etwas satt werden

⚠ Bei ***get*** liegt die Betonung auf dem (allmählichen) Veränderungsprozess.

Alternativ zu ***get*** gelegentlich auch das gehobenere ***grow (old/weak/dark)*** bzw. ***become (rich/ill).***

***go** oder **get?** Setzen Sie die passende Form ein.*

1. *My eyesight seems to have _________ worse since I've been working in front of a computer screen.*
2. *When I told him, he _________ pale and then very red. Then, as the truth began to sink in, he gradually _________ angry.*
3. *There must be some way of _________ rich quick and enjoying life before we _________ too old and sick to do so.*
4. *Why do you have to keep on reminding me that I'm _________ bald and _________ fat?*

wie

how? — **what … like?**

– ***How*** *is Helmut?*
– *I'm afraid he's not very well.*

– ***What's*** *Helmut* ***like****?*
– *He's too much of a flirt for my liking.*

Bei Personen:

How is Helmut?
(Wie geht es Helmut?)

What's Helmut like?
(Wie ist Helmut so? / Was ist Helmut für ein Typ?)

how? fragt nach der Gesundheit, dem Wohlbefinden

what … like? fragt nach dem Wesen/Typ, der Persönlichkeit

Sonst:

I hear you were in Chicago. How was it?
(Wie war der Aufenthalt für dich persönlich?)

I've never been to Chicago. What's it like?
(Wie ist die Stadt eigentlich so?)

how? fragt nach einem persönlichen, subjektiven Erlebnis

what … like? fragt nach allgemeinen, „objektiven" Tatsachen

Bei Dingen oder Ereignissen sind oft beide Alternativen möglich, je nachdem, ob die Betonung auf dem persönlichen Erlebnis *(how?)* oder auf der objektiven Beurteilung *(what … like?)* liegt:

How was the film? (Wie hat dir der Film gefallen?)
What was the film like? (Wie war der Film?)

Auf jeden Fall sollten Sie sich Folgendes merken:
bei Personen: ***how for health*** (= Gesundheit)

Bilden Sie Fragen: ***how?*** *oder* ***what … like?***

1. – ______________________________?
(your new cleaning lady)
– *She's very good.*

2. – ______________________________?
(Simon)
– *Oh, he's feeling much better, thanks.*

3. – ______________________________?
(Andrew's school report)
– *It wasn't too bad this time.*

4. – ______________________________?
(you)
– *I'm fine, thanks. And you?*

wissenschaftlich

scientific? **scholarly?** **academic?**

Not everybody's cup of tea

*You call that a **scholarly piece of work**, do you? I call it a mess. And you say you want to go in for a university career and devote yourself to **academic research**. Well, you'll have to develop a more scholarly approach than this, I'm afraid. At least you're not planning on being a scientist. I can just see you blowing up a chemistry lab with some **scientific experiment**. If you really want my advice, stick to weightlifting.*

---

not everybody's cup of tea – nicht jedermanns Sache ***devote o.s. to s.th.*** – sich einer Sache widmen ***research*** – Forschung ***approach*** – Einstellung ***blow up*** – in die Luft jagen

Allzu wissenschaftlich wollen wir es hier nicht treiben, sondern Ihnen einfach ein paar Tipps geben, damit Sie mit diesem wirklich verzwickten Wortfeld besser zurechtkommen.

scientific

1. naturwissenschaftlich
   It gets more and more difficult to keep up with scientific developments these days.
2. wissenschaftlich genau / hieb- und stichfest
   Is there any scientific proof of a link between ozone levels and asthma attacks?

scholarly

gelehrt-wissenschaftlich; betont positiv die Methode einer Arbeit, des Denkens usw.

She has a very scholarly mind. I think she'll probably go into research of some sort.

academic

wissenschaftlich/geistig/intellektuell/akademisch, besonders im Zusammenhang mit der Universität und mit Publikationen
an academic career/discussion/institution/publisher/library
academic publications, the academic world
Why do so many academics have to write in such a highly academic style that nobody can understand what they're talking about?

Übrigens:

science	(ohne Artikel) die Wissenschaft; die Naturwissenschaft(en)
the (natural) sciences	die Naturwissenschaften
arts and sciences	Geistes- und Naturwissenschaften
the arts, the humanities	die Geisteswissenschaften
research	die Forschung, die Wissenschaft
researcher	Forscher, Wissenschaftler

scientific, scholarly *oder* ***academic?***

1. *He's thinking of an ________________ career – a job at university or some other institute of higher education.*

2. *Lack of funds for ________________ experiment and research is driving Britain's top physicists to other countries in a massive brain drain.*

3. *One of our main aims is to develop a ________________ and balanced way of thinking among our students.*

---

brain drain – Abwanderung von Wissenschaftlern/Experten

Zuschauer

spectators? **audience?** **viewers?**

Give me a desert island

I enjoy watching football matches, but the rough behaviour of so many of the ***spectators*** *always frightens me. Going to the cinema just gets on my nerves – those people in the* ***audience*** *who eat their popcorn noisily, repeat all the jokes, and constantly get up to fetch more snacks and drinks – the way I imagine* ***TV viewers*** *to behave within their own four walls. At least at the theatre the* ***audience*** *has to sit still until the interval, though there are always those annoying people who cough loudest or rustle their sweet papers during the most dramatic parts. Well, I must be off to that demonstration at the town hall. Why on earth did I have to choose crowd psychology as my research topic?*

---

desert island – einsame Insel ***rustle*** – rascheln mit ***sweet paper*** – Bonbonpapier ***town hall*** – Rathaus ***crowd psychology*** – Massenpsychologie ***research topic*** – Forschungsthema

spectators

(auch ***crowd***) Zuschauer bei einer Sportveranstaltung
spectator sport – Zuschauersport
There weren't many spectators / There wasn't much of a crowd at the match on Saturday.

audience

1. Publikum/Zuschauer im Theater
   somebody in / a member of the audience – ein(er der) Zuschauer
   Somebody in the audience was snoring during the third act.
2. Publikum im Kino
   somebody in the audience – ein Zuschauer
   people in the audience – (einige) Zuschauer

viewer

(Fernseh-)Zuschauer; im Plural auch ***audience***
The number of viewers at peak hours on Thursday nights has dropped drastically since the soap opera finished.

---

peak hours – Spitzenzeiten ***soap opera*** – „Seifenoper", meist niveaulose Unterhaltungsserie

spectators, audience *oder* ***viewers?***

1. *"How many ______________ were there at the Cup final?" – "Oh, there must have been a crowd of about 100,000."*
2. *If enough ______________ refused to pay their licence fee, the standard of TV programmes might improve.*
3. *How did the ______________ react to that horrible scene at the beginning of the play?*

Cup final – Pokalfinale ***licence fee*** – Fernsehgebühren

Britisch versus amerikanisch

English as a world language?

Mr Wilson's aunt, who has lived in California for forty years, is spending a few weeks in London with her relatives. One place she wasn't planning on visiting is the police station ...

Police Officer: *So you've lost your purse, Madam. Have you any idea where you might have lost it?*
Aunt Lizzie: *Well, I'd just been to* ***the movies*** *at Piccadilly, and then I went to a* ***drugstore*** *to get ...*
Police Officer: *A drugstore?*
Aunt Lizzie: *Yes, I needed something to clear my head after two hours in the* ***movie theater****. I wonder if I dropped my* ***purse*** *on the* ***sidewalk*** *as I was coming out of the* ***store*** *... You see, I noticed it was gone when I was standing in the bus* ***line****.*

Police Officer: *Could you tell me what was in the purse?*
Aunt Lizzie: *There was my **driver's license**, some **cookies** for when I get hungry, a book for the **subway** …*
Police Officer: *The subway?*
Aunt Lizzie: *Yes, it's one of the few chances I get to read. Then there was my **wallet**, of course, with about £50 in cash and my credit cards …*
Police Officer: *Your wallet?*
Aunt Lizzie: ***Sure**. Where else would I keep it? And a small **package** I was going to **mail** to my husband in Santa Barbara – he just loves English **candies**.*
Police Officer: *Well, I know everything's supposed to be bigger and better in the United States, but that really takes the biscuit.*
Aunt Lizzie: *Biscuit?*

---

that takes the biscuit – das schlägt ja alles (die Amerikaner sagen für „Keks" ***cookie*** statt ***biscuit***)

Es wird Ihnen vielleicht aufgefallen sein, dass die unterstrichenen Wörter amerikanische Ausdrücke sind, die den armen Londoner Polizeibeamten zum Teil ganz verwirrt haben. Zum Beispiel heißt *purse* im britischen Englisch „Portemonnaie", während es im Amerikanischen eine Handtasche bezeichnet, und die fallen ja etwas größer aus als der übliche Geldbeutel …

Die anderen Missverständnisse werden Ihnen anhand der nachstehenden Liste klar werden, die einige der geläufigeren Unterschiede im britischen und amerikanischen Wortschatz aufführt. Ausdrücke aus dem Dialog sind durch halbfette Schrift gekennzeichnet. Die mit einem Sternchen (*) gekennzeichneten „Amerikanismen" beginnen auch in Großbritannien allmählich Fuß zu fassen – ein Zeichen dafür, dass durch die heutige weltweite Kommunikation immer mehr amerikanisches Wortgut seinen Weg über den Atlantik findet.

britisch	*amerikanisch*	
biscuit	**cookie, cooky**	Keks
sweet	*candy*	Bonbon
jam	*jelly*	Marmelade
crisps	*potato chips*	Chips
chips	**(French) fries*	Pommes frites
trousers	*pants*	Hose
zip	*zipper*	Reißverschluss
shop	***store**	Geschäft
chemist's	*pharmacy*/**drugstore**	Apotheke
cinema	**movie theater**	Kino
go to the cinema	*go to the movies*	ins Kino gehen
film	**movie*	Film
bill	*check*	Rechnung (im Restaurant)
(bank)note	*bill*	Geldschein
handbag	**purse**	Handtasche
purse	**wallet**/*coin purse*	Portemonnaie
wallet	*billfold*	Brieftasche
petrol	*gas/gasoline*	Benzin
driving licence	**driver's license**	Führerschein
motorway	*highway/freeway/ expressway*	Autobahn
boot	*trunk*	Kofferraum
bonnet	*hood*	Kühlerhaube
windscreen	*windshield*	Windschutzscheibe
accelerator	*gas pedal*	Gaspedal
hire a car	*rent a car*	ein Auto mieten
taxi	**cab*	Taxi
railway	*railroad*	Bahn
rails	**tracks*	Gleis(e)
public transport	*public transportation*	öffentliche Verkehrsmittel
pavement	**sidewalk**	Bürgersteig

* ***Diese Wörter werden Sie auch im britischen Englisch finden.***

britisch	*amerikanisch*	
underground	**subway**	U-Bahn
subway	**(pedestrian) underpass*	Fußgängerunterführung
queue	***line**	Schlange
city centre	*downtown*	City, Innenstadt
flat	*apartment*	Wohnung
ground floor	*first floor*	Erdgeschoss
lift	*elevator*	Aufzug
cloakroom	*checkroom*	Garderobe
cupboard	*closet*	Schrank
toilet	*bathroom/rest room*	WC
tap	*faucet*	Wasserhahn
nappy	*diaper*	Babywindel
torch	*flashlight*	Taschenlampe
rubbish	**garbage/trash*	Abfall
rubber	**eraser*	Radiergummi
timetable	**schedule*	Fahrplan
postbox	*mailbox*	Briefkasten
parcel	***package**	Päckchen, Paket
send	***mail**	schicken
holiday	*vacation*	Urlaub
autumn	*fall*	Herbst
sorry	*excuse me*	Entschuldigung!
pardon?/sorry?	*excuse me?*	Wie bitte?
of course	***sure**	(Aber) Natürlich!

**** Diese Wörter werden Sie auch im britischen Englisch finden.***

„Falsche Freunde“

Wir alle kennen sie, die so genannten „falschen Freunde“: deutsche und englische Wörter, die auf den ersten Blick eng miteinander befreundet zu sein scheinen, in Wirklichkeit aber wenig miteinander zu tun haben, ja manchmal sogar das genaue Gegenteil ausdrücken können. Versuchen wir, ein paar der heimtückischsten zu demaskieren:

Angst haben

Some pupils are scared to go home with their school reports because they have such bad marks. Sometimes I feel quite anxious about these poor kids and the pressure their parents put them under.

be scared/frightened/afraid (of) – Angst haben (vor)

be/feel anxious about – besorgt sein um
be anxious to – darauf bedacht sein zu

bekommen

All I got for the article I wrote was five free copies of the magazine. I'm not really sure whether I'm on the right road to becoming rich and famous.

get, be given, receive – bekommen

become – werden (siehe auch **werden** im Hauptteil)

(sich) blamieren

"Whenever we go out together he always makes a fool of himself, and shows me up at the same time."
"Well, you only have yourself to blame – we all warned you against marrying him."

show s.o. (o.s.) up – jd. (sich) blamieren
make a fool of s.o. (o.s.) – jd. (sich) lächerlich machen

⚠ ***blame s.o.*** – jdm. die Schuld geben

Brieftasche

I had put my wallet with all that money into my briefcase because you can lock it. Then, stupidly, I left my briefcase on the train.

wallet – Brieftasche

⚠ ***briefcase*** – Aktentasche

Chips

"Do you remember the days when there used to be a little blue bag of salt in every packet of crisps?"
"Oh yes. And I also remember eating fish 'n' chips out of newspaper. Times have certainly changed."

crisps – (Kartoffel-)Chips [Am. *potato chips*]

⚠ ***chips*** – Pommes frites [Am. *(French) fries*]

engagiert

He used to be a very committed politician. But since he's been engaged to that fashion model he seems to have his mind on other things.

committed – engagiert
be very involved in politics – politisch engagiert sein

⚠ ***engaged*** – 1. verlobt; 2. (Telefon, Toilette) besetzt

eventuell

He says he <u>might possibly</u> be home by eight tonight, but he's always late. And even when he does eventually get back from work, he usually falls straight asleep on the sofa.

possibly – eventuell

*"Will you do it?" – **"I might."*** – … „Eventuell."
I might consider doing it – ich würde es eventuell machen

⚠ ***eventually*** – schließlich (= nach längerer Zeit/Mühe)

Karton

Could you fetch me one of those <u>cardboard boxes</u> from over there, please. I can't get all these cartons of milk into the shopping bag.

(cardboard) box, (kleiner) ***shoebox*** – Karton

carton of milk – Milchtüte
⚠ ***carton of orange juice*** usw. – Packung Orangensaft usw.
carton of cigarettes – Stange Zigaretten

Menü

I don't really fancy the <u>set lunch</u>. I think I'd better have a look at the menu and order à la carte.

set meal, set lunch – Menü

⚠ ***menu*** – Speisekarte

Note

See this fifty-pound note? If your <u>marks</u> in French and Geography improve by the end of term, it's yours.

mark/(bes. Am.) ***grade*** – Schulnote

⚠ ***note*** – 1. Geldschein [Am. *bill*]; 2. Musiknote

Fantasie

Well, he's certainly got plenty of <u>imagination</u> – all these fantasies he has about writing a best-seller, getting rich and buying an island in the Pacific.

imagination – Fantasie, Vorstellungskraft

⚠ ***fantasy*** – fantastische Vorstellung, Vision

💡 <u>***fantasy***</u> ist immer etwas <u>Fantastisches</u>

psychisch

Now she claims she's got psychic powers and can communicate with the dead. I know she's always had <u>psychological</u> problems, but if it goes on like this she'll end up as a <u>mental</u> case.

psychological – psychisch
mental – **1.** psychisch; **2.** geisteskrank

⚠ ***psychic*** – übersinnliche Kräfte besitzend, hellseherisch

Rückseite

He's stuck the stamp on the <u>back</u> of the envelope! Sometimes I feel like giving him a kick in the backside.

back – Rückseite

⚠ ***backside*** – Hintern

"I wrote it on the backside."

selbstbewusst

My new assistant's such a self-confident young lady and really knows what she's talking about. I have a feeling the others in the department feel quite self-conscious when she's around.

self-confident – selbstbewusst

⚠ ***self-conscious*** – befangen, gehemmt, unsicher

sensibel

"Don't keep criticizing his English – he's very sensitive."
"Well, if he was sensible about it he'd spend more time with his books so that he wouldn't make so many mistakes."

sensitive – sensibel, empfindlich

⚠ ***sensible*** – vernünftig

starten

"We'd better set off for the airport now if we want to catch our flight."
"Yes, I remember the last time we got to Heathrow just as our plane to Toronto was taking off…"
"All right, let's not start that business again."

set off – starten, losfahren, abreisen
take off – (Flugzeug) starten

⚠ ***start*** – beginnen (mit), anfangen (mit)

Studium

She takes her studies very seriously – she spends most of her time upstairs in her Dad's study buried in a pile of books.

(course of) studies, degree – Studium, Studiengang
a degree in physics – ein Physikstudium (usw.)

⚠ ***study*** – 1. Arbeitszimmer; 2. spezifische Untersuchung; 3. Erforschung

sympathisch

Our new neighbour seems a very likeable sort of person. And he was very sympathetic when our dog died last week.

likeable, very pleasant, nice, personable – sympathisch

⚠ ***sympathetic*** – 1. mitfühlend; 2. verständnisvoll

überhören

"I missed that – did he say he was going into retirement?"
"I didn't catch it either, it's so noisy in here. But I did overhear him saying to Mark yesterday that he's had enough of this company."

miss, not catch – überhören

⚠ ***overhear*** – zufällig (mit)hören, mitbekommen, „aufschnappen"

übernehmen

When he takes over his father's company, he'll have overtaken us all on the income scale.

take over – übernehmen

⚠ ***overtake*** – (auch im Verkehr) überholen

Unternehmer

He started off as an undertaker with a very small business. Now he's teamed up with a clever businessman and has himself become a successful entrepreneur with a worldwide market for exclusive animal coffins.

entrepreneur, (big) businessman – Unternehmer
industrialist – industrieller Unternehmer

⚠ ***undertaker*** – Leichenbestatter

Warenhaus

I had hoped to be able to pick up a bookcase at the department store, but they had most of their furniture in the warehouse, so I had to drive all the way out of town to get it.

department store – Warenhaus

⚠ ***warehouse*** – (Waren-)Lager

sich wundern

I was surprised to see her with Tony all of a sudden. I wonder if she and Paul have split up.

be surprised – sich wundern

⚠ ***wonder*** – sich fragen

I wonder if – ich würde ganz gern wissen, ob

Holen Sie noch einmal tief Luft: Es kommt nun der allerletzte, dafür etwas ausführlichere Test. Übersetzen Sie das Deutsche in Klammern:

1. *Let me see what's written on the* ______________ (Rückseite) *of that photo.*
2. *You have to watch what you say to her – she's very* ______________ (sensibel).
3. *When are we going to* ______________ (übernehmen) *this company and shake it up a bit?*
4. *"Are you coming to the reading by Salman Rushdie?" – "*______________ (eventuell).*"*
5. *What* ______________ (Note) *did he get in English?*
6. *I need some strong* ______________ (Kartons) *to pack all these books into.*
7. *He's the kind of model* ______________ (Unternehmer) *Mrs Thatcher always used to praise.*
8. *Try not to* ______________ (uns blamieren) *again this time.*

9. *If you haven't got a recipe for stew, just use your* ______________ (Fantasie).

10. *Do you think you could crunch your* ______________ (Chips) *a bit more quietly, please.*

11. *You really shouldn't keep both your cheque card and your cheques in your* ______________ (Brieftasche).

12. *The* ______________ (Menü) *looks quite interesting, and it's fairly cheap – shall we take that?*

13. *He's incompetent and thick, and yet he goes around with such a* ______________ (selbstbewusst) *air.*

14. *A fire broke out at one of the* ______________ (Warenhäuser) *in the pedestrian precinct last night.*

15. *The new head of personnel doesn't seem to be very* ______________ (sympathisch).

16. *How much did you* ______________ (bekommen) *for your Skoda?*

17. *What we need is more* ______________ (engagiert) *employees who are prepared to do overtime.*

18. *A lot of the patients with severe* ______________ (psychisch) *disorders started off with quite minor* ______________ (psychisch) *problems.*

19. *I'm afraid I* ______________ (überhörte) *most of the figures she was quoting.*

20. *After two* ______________ (Studiengänge), *don't you think it's time you got down to some real work?*

21. *Everyone* ______________ (hat sich gewundert) *to see me back from my skiing holiday so soon.*

22. *Why* ______________ (hast du Angst) *to ask him?*

23. *The hijacked plane is due to* ______________ (starten) *for Athens in half an hour.*

Schlüssel zu den Übungen

A. Typische Fehler von A – Z

aufstehen: 1. get up; 2. stand up
Bank: 1. bench; 2. bank; 3. benches
bemerken: she **noticed** me; she loudly **remarked**
bequem: 1. convenient; 2. comfortable; 3. lazy; easy; 4. easy
besondere(r,-s): something **special**; one **particular** video camera; a **special** price
besuchen: 1. go to; 2. attend; 3. go and see; 4. visit
bis (zu): 1. by; 2. until; 3. By the time
Boden: The **ground**; the living-room **floor**
brauchen: 1. I need a tie for the wedding. 2. It only takes him ten minutes to type a page. 3. How long did it take you to get here?
bringen: 1. took; 2. bring/get; 3. bring
Chef: 1. chef; 2. boss
dick: much too **fat**; a **thick** book; that **thick**
eng: 1. cramped; 2. close; 3. tight; 4. narrow
erkennen: 1. realize; 2. recognize
erst: 1. Lunch won't be ready until two. 2. The cheque only arrived the day before yesterday. 3. He won't be fifty until next year. 4. They've only won one game/match (so far).
fahren: **going** for; how to **travel**; **go** by train; like **driving**; **travel** long distances; be **driven** around
Fehler: a **fault**; so many **mistakes**; the **mistakes**; printing **errors**; a character **flaw**
fertig: 1. **Have** you **finished**; 2. **Are** you **ready**; 3. when you **have finished**; 4. **Are** you **ready**
Frau: so many **women**; my **wife**; a really elegant **lady**; a very intelligent **woman**
Fremder: 1. stranger; 2. foreigners; 3. strangers
Freund(in): a new **boyfriend**; He's a **friend**; a steady **girlfriend**

früher: **1.** We used to have three dogs. **2.** You never used to be so funny. **3.** In the past there were a lot more monarchies in Europe. / (In the past) There used to be a lot more monarchies in Europe.

Garderobe: **1.** hallstand; **2.** cloakroom; **3.** dressing-room

glücklich: **1.** happy; lucky; **2.** lucky; happy; **3.** lucky

groß: **1.** big; **2.** large; great; **3.** tall

Haare: **1.** hair; hairs; **2.** hair; **3.** hairs

hören: **Listen!**; **hear** that noise; **hear** a thing; **listen to** the late-night news; **hear** another word

kennenlernen: first **met**; **get to know** each other

klein: **1.** little; **2.** small; **3.** small; **4.** little

kochen: **1.** boil; **2.** making; **3.** cooked

kontrollieren: **1.** check; control; **2.** control; **3.** checked; **4.** checked

krank: **1.** ill; **2.** sick; **3.** ill; **4.** sick

Kritik: your **criticism**; their **reviews**

Kurve: **1.** bends; **2.** curve; **3.** corners

Land: **1.** country; **2.** Land; Land; **3.** countries; **4.** land; country

Landschaft: **1.** landscape; **2.** countryside; **3.** scenery

lassen: **1.** leave; **2.** let; **3.** leave; **4.** let

laut: **1.** noisy; **2.** loud; noisy; **3.** loud

leicht: **1.** slight; **2.** light; **3.** slight; **4.** easy

leihen: I **borrowed**; **lend** me; **lent** something; I **borrowed**

lernen: **studying/revising** again; I've been **revising**; I had to **learn**; and **revise**; **learnt** very much

lustig sein: **1.** funny; **2.** fun; **3.** fun; funny

machen: **1.** making; doing; **2.** do; do; **3.** go on; do; went on; do/take; taken

meinen: **1.** think; **2.** mean; mean; think; **3.** think

merken: **1.** notice; **2.** realize; **3.** noticed; realized

Müll: **1.** waste; **2.** rubbish; **3.** refuse/rubbish

nächste(r,-s): the **nearest** oasis; the **next** acacia tree; the **next** oasis

in der Nähe (von): **near** the race track; house **nearby**; **near** there; **nearby** comprehensive school

Natur: **1.** countryside; **2.** natural environment; **3.** nature; **4.** natural surroundings/nature

Paar: **1.** couple; **2.** pair

passen (zu): **suits** you; **goes with** your hair; **matches** your new beach towel; **fit** you

Pause: 1. interval; 2. breaks; 3. breaks
Platz: a **space**; their proper **place**; plenty of **room**
Reise: 1. trip; 2. journey; 3. trip; voyage
Rezept: 1. recipe; 2. prescription; 3. recipe
ruhig: Be **quiet**; sit **still**; stay **calm**
sagen: 1. says; 2. told; 3. told; said
Salat: salad; lettuce
Schatten: 1. shadows; 2. shade
schwer: getting **hard**er; a **heavy** lorry; very **difficult**
See: 1. lake; 2. sea; 3. Lake
seit: **for** a long time; **since** 1981; **for** years; **since** he was 14; **since** the pub opened
so: **so** self-confident; **such** a lot; **such** an idiot; goes on **like this**
sportlich: an **athletic** person; some **sporting/sports** event; a **sporty** type; a bit more **sporting**
stören: 1. bother; disturb; 2. bother; 3. spoiling
Straße: 1. road; 2. street; 3. road; 4. street
streng: the **strict** schoolmaster; a **severe** expression; less **severe**; **strict** discipline
Technik: when it comes to **technical matters**; special **technique**; modern **technology**; the latest **technology**; electrical **engineering** degree
Termin: 1. deadline; 2. appointments; 3. date
tödlich: 1. lethal/deadly; 2. fatal; 3. deadly/fatal
tragen: 1. wear; carry; 2. wearing; 3. wear; carry
Treppe(n): 1. stairs; 2. steps; 3. stairs
Übung: 1. exercises; 2. practice; 3. exercise
verboten: 1. prohibited; 2. not allowed; 3. forbidden
während: 1. while; during; 2. During
wenn: 1. If; 2. when; 3. If
werden: 1. got; 2. went; got; 3. getting; get; 4. going; getting
wie: 1. What's your new cleaning lady like? 2. How's Simon? 3. What was Andrew's school report like? 4. How are you?
wissenschaftlich: 1. academic; 2. scientific; 3. scholarly
Zuschauer: 1. spectators; 2. viewers; 3. audience

„Falsche Freunde“

1. back; 2. sensitive; 3. take over; 4. I might/Possibly; 5. mark/grade; 6. boxes/cardboard boxes; 7. businessman/entrepreneur; 8. show us up/make a fool of us; 9. imagination; 10. crisps; 11. wallet; 12. set lunch/set meal; 13. self-confident; 14. department stores; 15. likeable/pleasant/nice/personable; 16. get; 17. committed; 18. mental; psychological; 19. missed/didn't catch; 20. degrees; 21. was surprised; 22. are you scared/frightened/afraid; 23. take off

Register

a

b

c